SIMCHAH

A SHAAR PRESS PUBLICATION

IT'S NOT JUST HAPPINESS

RABBI ABRAHAM J. TWERSKI, M.D.

FIRST EDITION
First Impression . . . November 2006

Published and Distributed by
MESORAH PUBLICATIONS, Ltd.
4401 Second Avenue
Brooklyn, New York 11232

Distributed in Europe by
LEHMANNS
Unit E, Viking Business Park
Rolling Mill Road
Jarrow, Tyne & Wear NE32 3DP
England

Distributed in Australia & New Zealand by
GOLDS WORLD OF JUDAICA
3-13 William Street
Balaclava, Melbourne 3183
Victoria Australia

Distributed in Israel by
SIFRIATI / A. GITLER — BOOKS
6 Hayarkon Street
Bnei Brak 51127

Distributed in South Africa by
KOLLEL BOOKSHOP
Ivy Common 105 William Road
Norwood 2192, Johannesburg, South Africa

THE ARTSCROLL SERIES®
SIMCHAH: IT'S NOT JUST HAPPINESS
© Copyright 2006, by MESORAH PUBLICATIONS, Ltd.
4401 Second Avenue / Brooklyn, N.Y. 11232 / (718) 921-9000 / www.artscroll.com

---

No part of this book may be reproduced
in any form *without* **written** *permission from the copyright holder,*
except by a reviewer who wishes to quote brief passages in connection with a review
written for inclusion in magazines or newspapers.

THE RIGHTS OF THE COPYRIGHT HOLDER WILL BE STRICTLY ENFORCED.

ISBN-10: 1-4226-0218-4 / ISBN-13: 978-1-4226-0218-8 (h/c)
ISBN-10: 1-4226-0219-2 / ISBN-13: 978-1-4226-0219-5 (p/b)

Printed in the United States of America by Noble Book Press Corp.
Bound by Sefercraft Quality Bookbinders, Ltd., Brooklyn, N.Y.

Table of Contents

	Introduction	7
1.	Simchah — the Foundation of Mitzvos	15
2.	What Is Simchah?	19
3.	Simchah — Not Only Joy	28
4.	Coexistence of Simchah and Sadness	32
5.	The Power of Simchah	39
6.	Attaining Simchah	42
7.	All "Simchas" Can Lead to Joyous Simchah	48
8.	Simchah and the Family	50
9.	Shabbos — the Holiness of Time	55
10.	Tefillah (Prayer)	67

11. Tzedakah and Gemilas Chassadim	76
12. Bircas HaMazon (Blessing After Meals)	83
13. Mezzuzah	89
14. The Shofar and Rosh Hashanah	92
15. Yom Kippur — a Fresh Start	97
16. Succos and the Four Species	101
17. Passover — A Prelude to Simchah	107
18. Counting of the Omer	112
19. Shavuos and the Torah	116
20. Chanukah — the Light of Judaism	120
21. Purim — The Greatest Miracle?	124
22. Rosh Chodesh (The New Month) — Renewal	128
23. Tzitzis — The Threads that Bind	131
24. Tefillin — Thought and Deed	134
25. Honoring Parents	140
26. The Chukim	143
27. Bris Milah (Circumcision)	146
28. Pidyon Haben (Redemption of the First-Born Son)	150
29. Marriage and Family	153
30. Emunah (Faith)	156
31. The Human Being — A Speaking Soul	160
32. Berachos (Blessings)	165
33. You Shall Be Holy	168
34. A Demeanor of Simchah	171
35. Doing What is "Fair and Good"	175
36. Middos	180
37. Does Mourning Negate Simchah?	195
Epilogue	198

Introduction

I was on my way to shul on the first day of Passover. A bit ahead of me, a young man was whistling as he walked his dog. Abruptly, he stopped, snapped his fingers, and whirled around in a merry dance.

It suddenly struck me. Just last night, I had performed several mitzvos. I had eaten the matzah and *marror*, drunk the four cups, and recited the Haggadah. Earlier in the day I had performed the mitzvah of disposing of *chametz*. I was on my way to shul to *daven* (pray) to Hashem. Yet, *I was not dancing*! What was wrong with me? I had fulfilled these precious mitzvos but I was not elated.

For that matter, I do mitzvos every day. I wear *tzitzis* and put on *tefillin*. I *daven* and *bentsch* (recite the blessing after meals). I give *tzedakah* and study the Torah, all precious mitzvos. Why am I not dancing with joy every day?

Could it be that my prayers are nothing but lip service? In the morning prayers I say, "How fortunate we are, how goodly is our portion, and how sweet is our lot. How fortunate that we can declare twice each day, '*Shema Yisrael,*' Hashem, our G-d, Hashem is One." If we really believe that this is our good fortune, why are we not euphoric? Where is my simchah?

Giving it a bit of further thought, it is not only the performance of specific mitzvos that should make me happy. After all, the most fundamental mitzvah is the belief in Hashem, the first of the Ten Commandments. Every time I utter the words, *"baruch Hashem"* (G-d is blessed; an expression of thanksgiving) or *"im yirtzah Hashem"* (G-d willing), I am asserting my belief in Hashem. Shouldn't the observance of this mitzvah bring me joy?

It was inescapable. I was grossly remiss in *simchah shel mitzvah*.

But can a person always be elated by performance of mitzvos? Perhaps there may be circumstances in a person's life that prevent one from feeling joy, even if one values mitzvos highly. As we shall see, there are aspects of simchah other than joy, and if we can achieve these, we may be able to experience the joy of mitzvos even when circumstances are not conducive to feeling joy.

Yes, many things may occur during a day that are stressful or unpleasant. But suppose I had won millions of dollars in the lottery. Would these things detract from my elation, or would I push them aside as being insignificant, hardly worth becoming upset over them? The Psalmist says, "I rejoice over Your word like one who has found a great treasure" (*Psalms* 119:162). Can it be that in spite of my observance of mitzvos, I do not appreciate their enormous value?

One might say, "How can you compare me with King David? As a king, he was free of the difficulties and stresses I experience. These constant pressures weigh heavily on me and do not allow me to experience the joy in mitzvos. If I was free of all worry, then I could feel the joy."

But was David indeed free of difficulties and stress? Let us see what David's life was like.

David grew up being looked down upon by his family.

In fact, when G-d instructed the prophet Samuel to anoint one of Yishai's sons as king, Yishai presented all of his sons except for David. He wasn't even thought a candidate. At G-d's behest, Samuel rejected each of Yishai's sons, and asked if there were others. Yishai replied that there was indeed one more, David. To everyone's surprise, David was the one chosen to be king of the Jewish nation.

Shortly thereafter, David slew Goliath and became a favorite of King Saul, who took him as a son-in-law. Saul then fell into a state of melancholy, persecuting David and seeking to kill him, so that David had to flee for his life. When Saul died in battle, David became king, but only two tribes, Judah and Benjamin, acknowledged him.

David's enemies continued to harass him, stating that as a descendant of a Moabite, he was not qualified for the kingship. Even when all tribes recognized David as king, the harassment did not cease. In *Psalms*, David complains bitterly how his enemies persecute him and how his bosom friends turned against him.

David never made peace with himself with regard to the Bathsheba incident, and suffered much agony because of it. Then, his son Absalom led a revolt against him, driving him from Jerusalem. In quelling the revolt, David ordered his general to spare Absalom and when the latter was killed, David was inconsolable. "My son, Absalom! My son, Absalom! Would that I would be dead rather than you" (*II Kings* 19:1). He lost another son Amnon, following the latter's inappropriate assault.

David lived to age 70, and according to the Midrash, *he did not have a single good day in his entire life*! Despite his intense and relentless suffering, David repeatedly expresses his simchah in *Psalms*. "You put gladness in my heart" (4:8). "For this reason my heart does rejoice and my soul is elated" (16:9)."I will rejoice in Hashem" (104:34). "I will rejoice and exult in You" (9:3). "We shall sing out and rejoice all our days" (90:14). The theme of simchah appears countless times in *Psalms*, expressed by a person who was never free of agony!

Granted, it is asking a great deal of a person. Yet, this is a basic tenet of *emunah,* to have faith and trust in Hashem, and to be able to tolerate adversity with a "complete heart." It was because David was able to do this that his suffering did not interfere with his *simchah shel mitzvah.* "Had Your Torah not been my preoccupation, I would have perished in my affliction" (*Psalms* 119:92). It was his unshakable faith that enabled him to say, "I rejoice over Your word like one who has found a great treasure" (*Psalms* 119:162).

Let me share something that I heard from a young woman in recovery from alcoholism and drug addiction. After relating the story of her decline due to her addiction and her subsequent recovery, she said, "There is one more thing I must tell you.

"I am a rabid football fan. The New York Jets are my team, and I will never miss a game. One weekend, I had to be away, and I asked a friend to record the game on her VCR. When I returned, she gave me the tape and said, 'By the way, the Jets won.'

"I began watching the game and I was horrified by the Jets' terrible performance. At half time, they were 20 points behind. Under other circumstances, I would have been a nervous wreck: anxious, pacing, and hitting the refrigerator for sweets to settle my nerves. But this time I was perfectly calm, because I knew the outcome; they were going to win.

"When I entered this recovery program, I made a conscious decision to turn my life over to the will of G-d. I know that eventually it will turn out all right, because G-d is in charge of my life. Sometimes, I am 20 points behind at half-time, but I don't panic. I know that I am ultimately going to win."

I felt chastened that I had to take a lesson in *bitachon* (faith and trust in G-d) from a recovering addict, but the Talmud says, "Who is wise? Someone who can learn from everyone" (*Ethics of the Fathers* 4:1), so my efforts to be wise triumphed over my pride. This lesson has often come to my rescue when experiencing adversity. Inasmuch as G-d is in charge, the outcome will ultimately be good, even though I cannot see this when I am 20 points behind.

True *bitachon* will allow us to experience *simchah shel mitzvah*. Such *bitachon* does not come naturally. It requires much work to achieve it. Perhaps this is what was meant by the verse, "*Ivdu es Hashem besimchah,*" which is usually translated as "Serve Hashem with gladness. As one Chassidic master pointed out, "*ivdu*" means "you shall work." One must put in appropriate effort and energy to achieve the *bitachon* that will enable one to have simchah.

I believe that the achievement of *simchah shel mitzvah* requires the understanding and implementation of simchah in its comprehensive sense; i.e., the variety of emotions over and beyond that of joy that are aspects of simchah. This will remove the barriers that obstruct the feeling of elation that should result from doing a mitzvah. This is what is meant by "Simchah — It's Not Just Happiness."

SIMCHAH
IT'S NOT JUST HAPPINESS

1

SIMCHAH — THE FOUNDATION OF MITZVOS

Yiddishkeit *is* simchah. Torah literature tells us that the ultimate goal of a Jew is to bond with Hashem, in this world as well as in the World to Come, and that the Divine presence cannot rest where there is *atzvus*. *Atzvus* is usually translated as "sadness," but as we shall see, this is not accurate.

Torah requires that we always maintain an attitude of simchah, yet there are times when sadness is actually proper, as on *Tishah B'Av* when we commemorate the loss of the *Beis Hamikdash* (Holy Temple) on *Tishah B'Av* or when one mourns the loss of a loved one. Inasmuch as the consensus of all *sifrei mussar* and *chassidus* is that there is never any place for *atzvus*, it cannot mean "sadness." For that matter, the translation of simchah as "joy" or "happiness" is not precisely accurate either, as we shall see. Simchah and *atzvus* cannot coexist, but contrary to what one may think, it is possible for a person to maintain simchah even when circumstances may justify feeling sad.

The pivotal role of simchah in Yiddishkeit can be seen from the statement in *Deuteronomy* (28:47), where, following the description of the terrible consequences that will befall the people of Israel if they should deviate from the word of Hashem, the Torah states that these will be because "you did not serve Hashem with simchah." The foremost deviation is, therefore, the failure to have simchah.

We customarily assume that deviance from Torah means committing sins such as violating Shabbos, eating *tereifah*, and the like. While these are indeed very grave sins, the great R' Chaim Vital says that the basis for all the mitzvos is *middos* (character traits), and that greater caution must be exercised in regard to *middos* than even to the positive commandments and prohibitions! (*Shaarei Kedushah* 1:2).

Nesivos Shalom (vol.1 p.300) elaborates on this, and quotes a Midrash that is nothing less than shocking, so much so, that I made sure to verify its authenticity. Midrash Tanchuma (*Eikev*) comments on the verse (*Deuteronomy* 7:7) "Not because you are more numerous than all the peoples did Hashem desire you and choose you, for you are the fewest of all the peoples." The Midrash says, "It is not because you do more mitzvos than them, because the other nations do more good deeds that they were not commanded, and they glorify My Name more than you, as is said (*Malachi* 1:11), 'From the rising of the sun until it sets, My Name is great among the nations, and everywhere they bring incense and pure *minchah* offerings to My Name, for My Name is great among the nations.' 'For you are the fewest,' but because you efface yourselves before Me, that is why I love you.' "

Nesivos Shalom marvels at the Midrash that says that the nations of the world do more mitzvos than Israel does and glorify His Name more than Israel, and it is only because Israel humbles itself before Hashem that He loves them. Even if other peoples do have more mitzvos, they lack self-effacement. In the section "The purity of *middos*" (*Nesivos Shalom* vol.1 pp. 75-104) the author points out that *middos* are the basis of Torah.

Some ask, "If *middos* are so important, why are they not explicitly stated in the Torah as mitzvos?" The answer to that is that just as a recipe book will list the ingredients necessary for a cake and the instructions how to combine them, it does not say, "Buy an oven," because it is assumed that one has an oven if one wishes to bake a cake. Similarly, the assumption is that a person has proper *middos* if he wishes to observe the Torah. As we will see, *middos* are what gives a human being his uniqueness and distinguishes him from other living things. A person must first and foremost be a *mentsch* in order to accept the Torah.

R' Ahron of Karlin says that a person must work on the development of simchah more than on any other of the *middos* (quoted in various Chassidic writings). If *middos* are the foundation of Yiddishkeit, and developing simchah is primary in *middos*, the inescapable conclusion is that simchah is not only an important ingredient in Yiddishkeit, but that Yiddishkeit *is* simchah.

But, you may say, simchah is an emotion. How can one be commanded to have an emotion? If circumstances are favorable and one is experiencing good fortune, one has simchah. On the other hand, if one is experiencing adversity, then one feels dejected, and it appears unrealistic to command a person to have simchah.

The Torah does not make unrealistic demands. The Creator's knowledge and understanding of man far surpasses that of philosophers and psychologists. "He fashions their hearts all together; He comprehends all their deeds" (*Psalms* 33:15). The fact that we think of simchah as a spontaneous response to propitious circumstances indicates that we do not understand the Torah concept of simchah. It is indeed an emotion, but it is an emotion that can be developed and that in actuality can coexist with feelings of sadness, albeit not with *atzvus*.

The primary *middos* that the Torah asks of us are *yiras Hashem* (awe and reverence of Hashem), *ahavas Hashem* (love for Hashem), and, as we have seen, simchah. Inasmuch as *yirah* is often thought of as being "fear," it is not too difficult to see how

1: Simchah — the Foundation of Mitzvos / 17

one can generate a fear of punishment. However, *ahavah* and simchah are subject to the question: How can a person be ordered to have an emotion? One either feels or does not feel something. One can be commanded to act or not to act in a certain way, but generating emotion seems to be beyond a person's ability. In the pages ahead, I will draw upon the writings of our sages and their life experiences to clarify why simchah is not a spontaneous response to circumstances, but can and should be cultivated.

Although the specific command in the Torah to have simchah is found only in regard to the celebration of the festivals (*Deuteronomy* 16:14), our *sefarim* extrapolate this to all the days of the year, based on the verse "Because you did not serve Hashem, your G-d, with simchah" (*Deuteronomy* 28:47). It is necessary, therefore, to know how this can be achieved. We will try to achieve this in the pages ahead.

WHAT IS SIMCHAH?

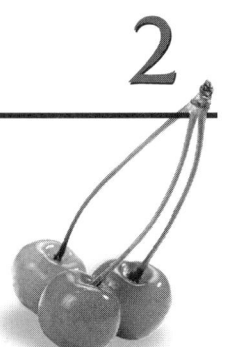

The clearest definition of a concept is often derived by contrasting it with its opposite. Thus, we can better understand heat as the opposite of cold and vice versa. We may better understand simchah by contrasting it with its opposite.

There were several stories that my father repeated a number of times. I am certain that this was because he wished to impress upon us the importance of the message conveyed by the story. One such story was about a man who had been sentenced to 25 years of hard labor. His wrists were shackled to the handle of a huge wheel that was set in the wall. All his waking hours he had to turn this massive wheel. He would often wonder what it was that he was doing. Perhaps he was grinding grain into flour or bringing up subterranean water to irrigate fields.

After the long sentence was completed and the shackles were removed, he ran to the other side of the wall. Upon seeing that the wheel was not attached to anything, he collapsed. Twenty-five years of backbreaking work, all for nothing! He was able to survive 25 years of bone-crushing labor, but the feeling that it was futile, all for naught, was more than he could bear.

Just as the most depressing feeling is futility, so the most elevating feeling is *accomplishment*. Yet, if one thinks of accomplishment in terms of a tangible achievement, one may be easily frustrated. The fact is that we have no control over outcome. We may plan something very carefully and execute our plan to the minutest detail, but factors beyond our control may prevent its coming to fruition.

Our culture is so entrenched in commercialism that our concepts of good and bad, right and wrong have been heavily influenced by commercial criteria. For example, a business that is successful and very profitable is a "good" business venture, even though the entrepreneur may have gone into the business carelessly and recklessly. If he reaped a windfall profit, even if his tactics were unethical or perhaps bordering on illegal, it was the right thing to do, and he is considered a shrewd businessman. If a person goes into a business venture with much careful planning, yet the business fails, it was the wrong thing to do and he is considered a poor businessman. Commerce is judged by the bottom line, and while this is appropriate for commerce, it has no place in one's personal and ethical life.

In contrast to commerce, a person's ethical life should be based on *process* and *method* rather than on results. For example, a greedy surgeon may perform an uncalled-for operation simply to collect a fee. As a result of the unnecessary surgery he discovers a tiny malignant tumor that he removes, thereby saving the patient's life. He is nevertheless an unscrupulous surgeon. On the other hand, a surgeon may have agonized about performing an operation on a patient with a life-threatening condition, which is generally correctable by surgery. However, for this patient, the operation has a considerable risk. After obtaining adequate consultation and giving it much thought, he decides that the patient's best chances for survival are with the surgery. Unfortunately, the patient dies. Yet, he is a dedicated and ethical surgeon. If one judges by outcome, the former surgeon is good and the latter is bad, but if one judges by method, the opposite is true.

The Chafetz Chaim cited the prayer that is said upon completion of a volume of Talmud. In this prayer, Torah scholars are contrasted with people who are devoid of Torah, and we read, "We (the former) toil and they (the latter) toil. We toil and are compensated, whereas they toil and are not compensated." The Chafetz Chaim asks, "Why do we say that people who are devoid of Torah are not compensated for their labor? Do we not pay workers for their work?"

The Chafetz Chaim answers, "We do not pay workers unless their work somehow results in a usable product. If a tailor were to work all day putting stitches in fabric that did not produce a garment, he would not be paid. Stitches that do not contribute to the formation of a garment are worthless. This is not so with Torah. There are some Torah laws that have never been applied and will never be applied, yet studying them is a mitzvah. There does not have to be an end product. Every word of Torah study is a mitzvah. That is how a Torah scholar differs from an artisan. His efforts are compensated even if they do not lead to a practical application."

In our prayers we regularly invoke the merits of the patriarchs, Abraham, Isaac, and Jacob. Hashem said, "I love Abraham because he will instruct his children and his household after him that they keep the way of Hashem" (*Genesis* 18:19). How successful was Abraham? He had eight sons (Isaac, Ishmael, and the children of Keturah), of whom only one followed the way of Hashem. If we go by outcome, Abraham was a failure. But, Hashem loved Abraham because his did his utmost, and it is by the process that we are judged.

How well did Isaac do? Of his two children, one was a *rasha*. 50 percent failure. Yet, we invoke the merit of Isaac because he was a *tzaddik* by virtue of his efforts. It is evident that a person is judged by what he does rather than by what he produces.

This is true of mitzvos and of every aspect of *avodas Hashem* (service of Hashem). The merit is in the *process* rather than in a fixed goal. The goal of life for a Jew, as explained in *Mesilas Yesharim* and chassidic writings, is to draw ever closer to Hashem. Inasmuch as Hashem is infinite, there is never an endpoint. One can never say, "I have reached Hashem." To the contrary, if one feels he has already arrived, he is more distant than ever.

One of the Baal Shem Tov's disciples complained of great frustration. "I try to draw myself closer to Hashem," he said, "but just when I feel a closeness, I am thrown back a distance."

The Baal Shem Tov explained with a parable. A father wished to teach his infant child to walk. When the child could stand upright, the father placed himself in front of the child, stretched out his arms, and beckoned to the child. Having always balanced himself on all fours, the child was fearful of taking a first step. However, seeing that his father was so close that he could catch him if he fell, the child felt safe in venturing the first step. The father then moved back a bit, and again beckoned to the child. Having taken a step without falling and seeing the father still close, the child has the courage to take two steps. The father then moves a bit farther back and continues retreating as the child advances.

The child must be thinking, *What is going on here? The more I try to reach my father, the farther away he goes!* What is happening here is that there are two disparate goals. The child's goal is to reach the father. The father's goal is to teach the child how to walk. The moment the father allows the child to reach him, the lesson is over and the growth process has come to an end.

"Your goal," the Baal Shem Tov said to the disciple, "is to reach Hashem. Hashem's goal is for you to grow spiritually by striving to reach Him. That growth would come to an end if Hashem allowed you to reach Him. Therefore, just as with the father and the infant, Hashem keeps moving back, so that you strive yet again to reach Him."

Thus, in contrast to most of our activities that have a finite goal, in *avodas Hashem* the process is the goal The contrast is even greater, because in our mundane activities in which we have a fixed goal, the process is actually burdensome. We may put in laborious effort to earn money because there is no other way to obtain it. If we could have the money without any effort, we would be delighted. We tolerate the process only because it is necessary to reach the goal, but we would gladly do without it. Just the reverse occurs in *avodas Hashem*, where the process is everything. As the Rebbe of Kotzk commented on the verse "From there you will seek Hashem, your G-d, and you will find Him" (*Deuteronomy* 4:29), "the seeking is the finding."

In our daily activities, we have many intermediate goals, but no ultimate goal. This is why we are never satisfied with earthly achievements. The Talmud says, "No one leaves this world having achieved even half of his desires" (*Koheles Rabbah* 1:34). People who are extremely wealthy and who have more money than they could consume in six lifetimes still continue to work to increase their wealth. There is no enduring satisfaction in achieving material aspirations. We have the pleasure of the moment, but it is evanescent, and we quickly pursue other pleasures.*

We often delude ourselves into thinking that we have ultimate material goals. R' Bunim of P'shihsche used to say, "Oh, where is that ultimate child?" He explained that he asks someone, "Why do you spend your entire day in an effort to earn money? Why don't you spend more time in prayer and Torah study?' The man responds, "Actually, my needs are rather meager. However, I must provide well for my child."

Eventually, that child grows up and he, too, spends the greater part of his time pursuing more income. When asked why he does not devote more time to spiritual pursuits, his answer is the same. He is not doing it for himself, but for his child. In an infinite

---

* In 1951, most homes did not have air-conditioning, and window units were expensive. It pained me to see how uncomfortable my father was in the sweltering heat. I borrowed money and installed an air-conditioner in his study. Fifty-five years later I can still savor the good feeling that I enabled my father to feel comfortable.

regress, one is always working not for oneself, but for "the child." Where, then, is the ultimate child for whom countless generations have been working?

It is characteristic of all intermediate goals that while their achievement may result in pleasure, that pleasure eventually wanes and one soon seeks additional pleasures. The enjoyment of a tasty dish is momentary, and just one hour after eating, that pleasure is gone. The pleasure of owning a new automobile may last for a number of days rather than minutes, but eventually the novelty wears off and it is just a vehicle. We may have an intense desire for something and we may feel that its acquisition will make us happy. However, if we will be truthful with ourselves, we will realize that this feeling is fleeting and that no earthly pleasure has endurance. We will realize the validity of King Solomon's statement, "What lasting gain does a person have from all his toil under the sun?" (*Ecclesiastes* 1:3). Our sages explain that "under the sun" refers to all earthly activities, none of which can provide more than fleeting satisfaction.

It is different with *avodas Hashem*. Because the process is the goal, every bit of *avodas Hashem* is an achievement. There is never any futility in *avodas Hashem*. Inasmuch as achievement brings about simchah, a life dedicated to *avodas Hashem* is a life of simchah.

Simchah shel mitzvah, as a component of *avodas Hashem*, goes beyond the actual performance of mitzvos. Everything that goes into the preparation for performance of mitzvos is *avodas Hashem*. Even the *thought* of doing a mitzvah is *avodas Hashem*. The Talmud says that the single verse upon which the entire Torah depends is "Know Hashem in all your ways" (*Berachos* 63a). This means that everything that one does should be directed toward *avodas Hashem*. Inasmuch as one cannot adequately do *avodas Hashem* unless one is in optimum health, everything one does to attain and preserve optimum health is part of *avodas Hashem*. Think of it! If you eat and sleep in order to have the energy for *avodas Hashem*, you are performing a mitzvah. If you need a bit of relaxation or judicious entertainment to function optimally, this too is *avodas Hashem*. You can actually be engaged in *avodas Hashem* 24/7/365. Is that not reason enough for simchah?

We can see that inasmuch as simchah is the polar opposite of futility, the opportunities for simchah are legion. If only we would give more serious thought to our purpose in life and discover that not only can we be goal directed in everything we do, but that every segment of *avodas Hashem* is actually a goal, we could permeate our lives with simchah.

We must differentiate between two types of simchah. An infant who gets the yellow ball it wants is happy. That is one kind of simchah. As we grow, our tastes become more sophisticated, and we are happy when we get a beautiful garment or a new automobile. But this kind of simchah is really only *quantitavely* different from that of the infant who gets the yellow ball. *Qualitatively*, it is the same feeling, and this type of feeling is dependent on the gratification of a desire. Yet, this is the simchah with which we are most familiar. This is the variety of simchah that is translated as "happiness." There is certainly nothing wrong with being happy or wanting to be happy, but simchah should not be restricted to this. Even the simchah of *nachas*, while it is certainly on a higher level than the acquisition of a desired object, is still the gratification of a desire.

Chassidic writings refer to the concepts of *moichin d'gadlus* (advanced intellect) and *moichin d'katnus* (juvenile intellect). Although the feeling on procuring a luxury automobile may appear to be a mature happiness, it is, in fact, *moichin d'katnus*. *Simchah shel mitzvah* goes beyond this, and while there can be a component of *simchah shel mitzvah* that is the pleasure of gratification, there is a qualitatively different simchah which is *moichin d'gadlus*. This type of *simchah* is attained only by dedicated effort. It requires the *ivdu*, the intellectual work to achieve it. As dignified, mature human beings, we should not be satisfied with what are essentially juvenile types of simchah, but should strive for a much higher, spiritual simchah.

That seeing happiness as being the satisfaction of a desire is juvenile was recognized by secular thinkers. "The kind of happiness many people have in mind is cheap and base — a vacuous state of 'bovine contentment' that cannot possibly be the basis of a meaningful human life" (R. Nozick, *The Examined Life* [New York: Simon & Schuster,1989], p. 102).*

That happiness as gratification of a desire cannot be the basis of a meaningful human life is illustrated by Charles Schulz in this cartoon.

Peanuts® by Charles M. Schulz. Reprinted by permission of United Features Syndicate, Inc.

The philosopher, John Stuart Mill, said, "It is better to be a human being dissatisfied than a pig satisfied; better to be Socrates dissatisfied than a fool satisfied. And if a fool or the pig are of a

---

* Albert Einstein said, "I have never looked at ease and happiness as ends in themselves—such an ethical basis I call more proper for a herd of swine." (*The World As I See It*, p. 2)

26 / *Simchah: It's Not Just Happiness*

different opinion, it is because they only know their own side of the question" (ibid.)

The ancient Athenian legislator, Solon, understood that true happiness is not the gratification of a desire. He said that one cannot say that a person was happy until the person's life had ended, because *happiness is the result of living up to one's potential* — and how can we make such a judgment until we see how the whole thing turns out?

Clearly, simchah is not limited to the colloquial meaning of happiness.

3

SIMCHAH — NOT ONLY JOY

Whereas the usual meaning of simchah is indeed "joy," it has other meanings as well.

The Talmud says that one must praise Hashem when experiencing adversity, just as one does when experiencing good things, and that one must do so with "simchah." The *berachah* to be recited is, "Blessed is the true Judge" (*Berachos* 60b). Rashi comments that in this case "simchah" means "*lev shalem* (with complete heart)." In other words, one should have complete faith and trust in the Divine justice, even though one may feel it to be unjust.

There were great *tzaddikim* who were actually able to feel content despite suffering because they felt that the adversity cleansed them from their "sins." A person who has his heart set

28 / *Simchah: It's Not Just Happiness*

on a beautiful diamond will gladly pay many thousands of dollars to acquire it. Although he sacrifices his money, he enjoys the transaction because what he receives is of greater value to him than the money. So it was with *tzaddikim*, who felt that the cleansing and forgiveness they were acquiring with their suffering was so dear to them that they gladly accepted the suffering.

However, most people are not at that level. Indeed, when tragedy strikes, the average individual must take refuge in the Talmudic statement that a person is not held culpable for his anger at Hashem when he is in great distress (*Bava Basra* 16b). When the acute pain has subsided, that is when a person should accept the Divine judgment with serenity.

Accepting adversity is certainly not easy. It is related that the great Talmudist, R' Zvi Chayis, was a well-to-do merchant. One day, when he was told that a ship laden with his merchandise sank at sea, he fainted. His students subsequently reminded him that he had taught them that one must praise Hashem when experiencing adversity just as one does when experiencing good things, and that one must do so with "simchah." R' Zvi responded, "I understood that Talmudic statement *al pi drash* (in theory) but not *al pi pshat* (practically)." One of the *gedolim (the Aderet, R' Avraham David Rabinowitz Tumim)* who lost a daughter did not come out to the funeral for several hours. He explained, "I must make the *berachah* 'Blessed is the true Judge.' I could not make this *berachah* wholeheartedly. I had to meditate for several hours until I could feel I was being truthful in stating that I was accepting Hashem's judgment with serenity."

It is enough of a challenge to deal with adversity when it happens. Many people, however, seem to have morbid expectations, anticipating that bad things may happen. Logically, there is no reason why one should feel this way. While it is true that unpleasant things occur in everyone's life, there really is no reason to anticipate misery.

I speak from experience, because for a long time I used to anticipate bad things. As an example, the hospital switchboard operator knew not to interrupt me when I was with a patient unless it was an emergency. One time, the operator interrupted to say that my son was on the phone. I froze, believing that, G-d forbid, something had happened in the family. When he was connected, he exclaimed, "Mazal tov!" I had just had another grandchild.

Didn't I know that my daughter-in-law was expecting a baby any day? Of course I did. Then why wasn't my first thought a pleasant one?

I knew that I was at the mercy of an irrational thought problem. I needed to reinforce my *bitachon*. I found the verse in *Psalms* (112:7), "Of evil tidings he will have no fear, his heart is firm, confident in Hashem." I say this psalm every day, not as a statement of fact but as a *tefillah* that it should be this way. This has been very effective, and I recommend daily recitation of Psalm 112 to people who have morbid expectations.

Some things may appear very unpleasant at the time they occur, but at a later date we can look back upon them and see them as being insignificant. Indeed, we may even laugh at them. I listed such incidents in *It's Not as Tough as You Think* and suggested that if the incident is something that we know we will laugh at five years down the road, why not laugh at it now?

There are other things that we may see as being very bad when they occur, only to later discover that they were "blessings in disguise." One woman said, "When I lost my job, I was very angry at G-d. 'What did I ever do to You to deserve this?' When my marriage broke up, I thought it was the end of the world for me. Now, years later, I am about to get a master's degree. I never could have done that if I had remained with that job. I can now see that my marriage was a very unhealthy relationship. I can see that G-d took away from me the things that I lacked enough sense to give up by myself."

The *tzaddik*, R' Baruch of Medzhibozh was reciting the prayer before *Kiddush* Friday night, and when he came to the verse, "I thank You for all the kindnesses You have done for me and for all the kindnesses You will do for me," he paused. "Why do I have to thank G-d now for future kindnesses? I can thank Him when they occur." Then he said, "Ah! I understand. I may not recognize His kindnesses when they occur, and may see them as being distresses." At that point he began crying. "How tragic! G-d will be doing kindness with me and I will not be able to recognize it."

The Midrash states that when the patriarch Jacob thought that Joseph had died, he complained that G-d had turned away from him, whereupon G-d said, "I am manipulating things to make his son viceroy of the largest empire on earth, yet he is complaining" (*Bereishis Rabbah* 91:13). There are many incidents that fall into this category.

Of course, there are things that we can never understand as being benign, and for these one can only accept them with what Rashi refers to as "with complete heart," i.e., with the belief that Hashem's justice is perfect, as Moses said, " The Rock! — perfect is His work, for all His paths are justice; a G-d of faith without iniquity, righteous and fair is He" (*Deuteronomy* 32:4).

Everything in our lives should be with simchah, whether the simchah of joy or the simchah of serenity.

4

COEXISTENCE OF SIMCHAH AND SADNESS

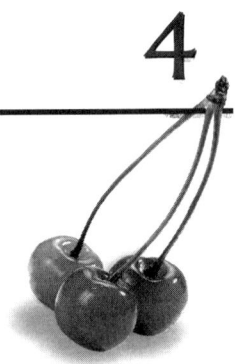

E arlier it was noted that *atzvus* does not mean sadness. *Tanya* (Chapter 31) states a psychological truth: *atzvus* means a total absence of feeling. "The heart is like stone." A person in the depth of depression is not sad. Rather, he has no feeling at all, except bitterness. It is a common psychiatric phenomenon that when a person is in a deep depression he may say, "I wish I could cry," and as he begins to recover, he may cry, because sadness is a return of feeling. The only sensation that a severely depressed person may have is bitterness. Indeed, the Hebrew word for this state is *marah shechorah*, which means "dark bitterness." Because a person in deep depression is unable to feel, he is inactive. He may despair of life and because he thinks that there is no hope, he does nothing. It is different when one is sad about something, because one may be motivated to do something to overcome the sadness. This is especially true if one feels the sadness associated with guilt for having sinned or for having been remiss in *avodas Hashem*. In contrast to *atzvus*, which paralyzes a person, this feeling is constructive because it stimulates a person to take corrective action. Awareness of this can be a source of simchah.

There was a case of a woman who was in a serious automobile accident in which she sustained multiple fractures. The fracture of her shoulder caused a tear in the nerves leading from the spinal cord to her right arm, so that the arm was without motion and without sensation. The surgeon reattached the nerve segments and told her that it would be several months before the success of the reattachment would be known, because it depended on the proper regrowth of the nerves. Her right arm was put in a sling and she had to wait patiently to see whether she would ever regain the use of her right hand.

Several months later, she was playing cards, and in her left hand held a cigarette together with the cards. In the process of moving the cards, the cigarette fell onto her right hand and she felt the burn. Excitedly, she threw the cards up and ran around the room, jumping for joy and exclaiming, "I'm hurting! I'm hurting!"

Usually, someone who sustains a painful burn is very upset. To this woman, the fact that she felt the pain of the burn was elating, because it meant that the nerves had grown properly and that she would regain the use of her right arm. Of what consequence was the pain compared to the knowledge that she would once again have the use of her right hand? The pain was a harbinger of a great good.

So it is with the painful awareness that one has done something wrong. This pain should be welcome, because it can lead to the corrective action of *teshuvah*.

This can be extended further. Assuming that simchah is the antonym of *atzvus* and that *atzvus* is, as *Tanya* says, the inability to feel, we come up with the conclusion that *the ability to feel* is a type of simchah. The importance of this can be appreciated if we can understand that many people try to avoid feelings. Classically, people who are addicted to alcohol, drugs, or food are using these substances as "tranquilizers" to escape uncomfortable feelings, whether they be anxiety, depression, or self-consciousness. Escaping from feelings is escaping from reality. Even addictions that do not involve substances, such as addictive gambling, are often an attempt to escape reality. We must learn how to deal with uncomfortable feelings so that we don't have to resort to escapist techniques.

The attempt to escape from painful feelings may sometimes result in *atzvus*, in a global lack of feeling. Let me share a case with you.

One day at the rehabilitation center, a therapist requested that I see one of his clients. "This fellow has been here for over two weeks," he said, "and he shows no signs of emotion at all. I wonder if he may have a psychiatric problem in addition to his addiction."

The young man was 28. He was very cooperative in the interview, but in discussing subjects in which some expression of emotion, any emotion, would be normal, there was nothing at all. Among the things he told me was that his father died suddenly when he was 10 years old. "I didn't cry. I looked at myself in the mirror and said 'You're not going to cry.' " In this interview, I did not see any sign of any specific psychiatric condition.

The next day, my wife told me that the faucet in the laundry sink was dripping. I am sufficiently handy to be able to change a washer, but to do so, I needed to turn off the water supply to the faucet. However, the valve was stuck, and I was afraid that if I forced it in an attempt to make it turn, I might break a pipe and flood the basement. There was no choice but to call a plumber.

But the plumber had no better luck than I did. He said, "This valve is frozen. It has probably never been turned since the house was built 75 years ago. The only thing I can do is shut off the main valve, but that will turn off the water supply to the entire house. It shouldn't be for more than 15 minutes."

A bit later the plumber came up holding the faucet. "You've got a problem, Doc," he said. "It's not the washer. The inside of the faucet is corroded. I'll have to replace the faucet."

"O.K.," I said. "There's not much choice."

"I have to go back to the shop to pick up a faucet," he said. "Your water will be off in the whole house for about two hours."

After the new faucet was installed and the main valve turned back on, the plumber opened the faucet, and a gush of rusty water came out with an explosive force and a loud noise. The plumber explained, "When the main valve was turned off, some air got in the pipes. The first time you open any faucet or shower or flush the toilet, you'll get an explosive discharge of water, but after that it'll be O.K."

It suddenly became clear to me what had happened with the young man. At age 10, he wanted to protect himself from the painful grief of his father's death. He did not know how to block the isolated emotion of grief, so he did what the plumber did. He shut off the "main valve," turning off *all* emotion. He could feel nothing. After being devoid of feelings for 18 years, he was afraid to feel anything, even pleasurable emotions. To allow himself now to feel *any* emotion, he would have to turn on the "main valve," but this might result in the emotion coming out with an explosive force that he felt he could not handle. Allowing himself to feel *any* emotion was too threatening, so he kept the "main valve" closed.

Once the problem was identified, we were able to help the young man, offering much reassurance and support to allow him to open his feeling system.

This insight has been very helpful to me. There are many people who seem to be devoid of emotion. This may be because of some occurrence that caused them to turn off their feeling system. If they cannot feel, they cannot have simchah.

Tishah B'Av is a sad day on which we mourn the loss of the Beis Hamikdash and our being driven into exile. It is related that when Napoleon heard of the observance of Tishah B'Av, he said, "A people who can mourn the loss of their sovereignty 2000 years ago are destined to regain it." The Greek and Roman empires once ruled the world. Who grieves for the loss of these empires today? They exist only in archaeological findings and in history books. Not so with the people of Israel. We have never forgotten Jerusalem, and we constantly express our hope and our belief that we will return to the glory of old. When the prophet Isaiah said, "Be glad with Jerusalem and rejoice in her, all who love her; exult with exultation, all who mourn for her" (66:10), he meant not only that they will rejoice in the restoration of Jerusalem with the ultimate Redemption, but that even as we mourn, there is reason for rejoicing. Napoleon was right. Our mourning for the loss of Jerusalem 2000 years ago indicates that it will be restored.

The Talmud relates that R' Akiva and several colleagues came across the ruins of the *Beis Hamikdash*. The colleagues wept, but R' Akiva smiled. He explained, "The two prophesies of the destruction of Jerusalem and its restoration are related. Seeing that the first has been fulfilled means that the second, too, will be fulfilled" (*Makkos* 24b).

R' Shmelke of Nikolsburg gave a parable about a king who was driven from his throne. As he went into exile, he stayed at the home of one of his officers. The officer was heartbroken to see the king in exile, but was thrilled that the king was his guest. We, too, are heartbroken that the *Shechinah* (the Divine Presence) has gone into exile, but we can nevertheless be happy that the *Shechinah* is with us.

There are times when an unpleasant happening should actually be reason for simchah, although we may not be able to appreciate it. There are times when simchah is the serenity of accepting Hashem's judgment, and there are times when we can be sad about something yet have simchah about something else. But there is never any time when one should be totally devoid of simchah.

We must at all times be grateful for the many kindnesses that Hashem bestows upon us. Because we are accustomed to life, we take it for granted and fail to see that life is a miracle. The Midrash says that we should thank Hashem for every breath (*Bereishis Rabbah* 14:11). We should be aware that we are the beneficiaries of Hashem's kindness.

After one terrorist attack in Israel, a person remarked that it was impossible to have simchah under these tragic conditions. A rabbi said to him, "Be truthful with yourself. If you had won six million *shekalim* in the lottery today, would the tragedy of the attack have prevented you from being happy over your winning?" The fact is that simchah and sadness can coexist.

The Baal Shem Tov once visited a town in which people complained that their *chazzan* (cantor) behaved strangely. On Yom Kippur, he would chant the *al chet* (confession of sins) with a merry melody rather than with the more appropriate solemn tune. When the Baal Shem Tov asked him to explain this, the *chazzan* said, "If I was the janitor in the king's palace and I was sweeping away the dirt, would I not be happy that I am beautifying the palace for the king? The *neshamah* within me is G-dly, and when I confess my sins I am cleansing myself to make myself a more pleasant dwelling place for the *neshamah*. Is that not good reason to rejoice?" The Baal Shem Tov praised this *chazzan* highly.

Sitting in a dentist's waiting room, I came across an article titled, "How Do Lobsters Grow ?" Come to think of it, how *can* a lobster grow? It is encased in an inflexible shell that does not expand.

The answer is that when the lobster grows, the shell becomes confining and oppressive. The lobster then retreats under a rock to be safe from predatory fish, sheds the shell, and produces a more spacious one. As the lobster continues to grow, the new shell eventually becomes oppressive, and the lobster will repeat the process of shedding the confining shell and producing a larger shell. This process is repeated until the lobster has reached its maximum growth.

The signal the lobster has that it's time to shed its shell so that it can continue to grow is *discomfort*! If lobsters had access to doctors, they might never grow. Why? Because when they felt the discomfort of the oppressive shell, they would get a prescription for a painkiller or a tranquilizer. With the discomfort gone, they would not shed the shell and produce a more spacious one. They would die as tiny little lobsters.

Of course, there are some emotional conditions that require

treatment, but very often, the feeling of discontent is not really a clinical depression. Rather, it is a signal that it is time to grow spiritually. Rather than being upset with this discomfort, we should welcome it, because without it, we might remain stagnant and never grow.

Yes, growth may be uncomfortable, but growth is closely related to simchah. R' Samson Raphael Hirsch states that when two Hebrew words are similar, they are related. *Some'ach* means "happy," and *tzome'ach* means "growth." "Happiness," R' Hirsch says, "is contingent upon growth."

The Talmud tells us about great *tzaddikim* who welcomed *yisurim* (suffering, *Bava Metzia* 84b). There is a story about a peasant who was accused of stealing from his master. Although he protested his innocence, the judge ordered that he receive 20 lashes. When the real thief was apprehended, the judge ordered that the master must compensate the peasant for his unjust punishment, and that he must pay him 10 rubles for each lash. The peasant then said to the judge, "Why did you only order 20 lashes? If you had ordered 50 lashes I could be much richer."

This story is applied to a person who stood before the Heavenly Tribunal on his judgment day. The prosecuting angels brought heaps of sins that he had done, and when the defending angels brought all the suffering he experienced, the latter were accepted as atonement and the number of sins were reduced. He then said, "How foolish I was to complain about my suffering! If I had suffered more, all of my sins could have been washed away."

While we may not reach the level of spirituality of those *tzaddikim* who actually welcomed suffering, we should be able to accept "growing pains" in the knowledge that we will thereby become better people.

The Power of Simchah

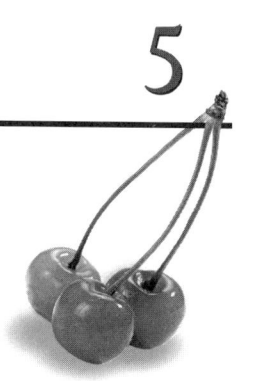

It is a common observation that when in a cheerful mood, one can accomplish much more than when one is morose. A person should not feel self-satisfied that he has done enough mitzvos, because the drawing closer to Hashem via mitzvos is never ending. To the contrary, study of Torah and performance of mitzvos results in one becoming aware of how much more there is yet to be accomplished. Nevertheless, said R' Levi Yitzchak of Berditchev, a person should be happy about the mitzvos one has done. Failure to be happy about mitzvos one has done indicates that one does not appreciate their great value.

The Ari *z"l* said that his enormous spirituality and monumental achievements were all due to the fact that he performed mitzvos with simchah. *Tanna DeVei Eliyahu* (Chapter 16) relates that the reason the prophet Isaiah, more than all other prophets, predicted Israel's return to its glory and greatness was because he accepted his mission with simchah. The Baal Shem Tov said that everything that can be achieved by fasting and self-denial can be achieved more quickly by doing mitzvos with simchah. R' Ahron Roth (*Shomer Emunim*) says that the *yetzer hara* directs all its forces to weaken a person's simchah, because this leads to negligence of mitzvos and greater vulnerability to sin.

R' Ahron cites a statement by the Maggid of Mezeritch that although tearful pleas to Hashem are meritorious, as the Psalmist says, "Hear my prayer, Hashem, listen to my outcry, be not mute to my tears" (*Psalms* 39:13), nevertheless praying with joy and singing the praises of Hashem is even more potent, because it elicits an outpouring of Divine *chesed* (benevolence).

The power of simchah is so great that it can have great force if it is used for evil. R' Levi Yitzchak of Berditchev says that the greatest danger that Haman posed was when he had simchah, as it says, "That day Haman went out joyful and exuberant" (*Esther* 5:9), because with simchah he could have achieved his evil plans. The turning point was when "Haman hurried to his home, despondent" (ibid. 6:12).

The Talmud relates that R' Ilai said to Ulla, "When you go up to Israel, greet my brother R' Beruna publicly. He is a great person and rejoices in the performance of mitzvos" (*Berachos* 9b), a quality that he held was as least as important as great Torah scholarship.

Chassidic writings state that all the obstacles to study of Torah and performance of mitzvos can be eliminated if one approaches Torah and mitzvos with simchah. R' Yaakov Yitzchak of P'shische cited the Talmudical statement that "although the heavenly gates of prayer are closed, the gates of tears are always open" (*Berachos* 32b) and said, "If the gates of tears were closed, tearful prayers could not enter, because they are said with sadness. However, prayers said with simchah can break through and penetrate even closed gates."

R' Tzadok cites the Talmudic statement that before Rabbah

would begin his Torah lecture to his students, he would tell them something to bring them to mirth (*Shabbos* 30b), and then would begin his lecture with an attitude of awe and reverence. The purpose of the introductory mirth was to stimulate a cheerful mind-set to increase their understanding of his Torah lecture (*Tzidkas HaTzaddik* 260).

It has been established in a number of studies that a cheerful attitude enhances recovery from disease. This is discussed at length in *The Anatomy of an Illness,* where the author describes how he "laughed his way" out of a serious illness. This was foretold by Solomon, "A man's spirit sustains him in sickness, but if his spirit is broken, who shall uplift it?" (*Proverbs* 18:14). R' Samson Raphael Hirsch comments, "A discontented, dissatisfied heart weakens the limbs and paralyzes activity, but good cheer brightens the outlook and straightens the body."

It is related that at the close of Yom Kippur, the Baal Shem Tov wished to recite the prayer of *Kiddush Levanah* (Sanctification of the New Moon), but the sky was covered with thick clouds. The Baal Shem Tov prayed fervently for the opportunity to say this prayer, but to no avail. His disciples, exuberant over the fact that Yom Kippur had erased all their sins, began to dance, and they pulled the Baal Shem Tov in to join them. Soon someone announced that there was a break in the clouds and that the moon was visible. Joyously, they recited *Kiddush Levanah.* The Baal Shem Tov said that what he was unable to accomplish with intense prayer was accomplished by his disciples with their simchah.

Of course, one must be cautious that simchah does not degenerate into levity, which may lead to improper behavior. But with this exception, there should be no restraints on simchah. It is good for both body and soul.

6
ATTAINING SIMCHAH

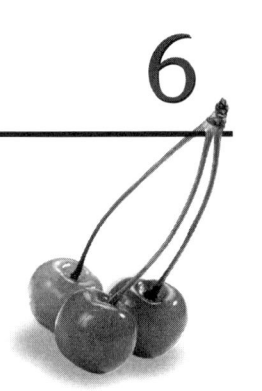

"**B**ut," one might argue, "simchah is an emotion. I'm either happy or not happy. How am I supposed to generate simchah?"

There are many things in *avodas Hashem* that require effort, and simchah is no exception. We must be diligent in the pursuit of simchah.

The *Sefer HaChinuch* makes a point that has been repeated by many ethicists. "A person's actions impact upon one's feelings" (Mitzvah 16). In other words, act as a happy person acts and you will feel happy. Modern psychology has embraced this principle. Earlier psychologic theories was that a person must change his inner feelings, which will then alter his behavior. Today the emphasis is on the converse. "Act the way you would like to feel and you will get to feel that way."

I was once sitting across the table from a psychiatrist at a convention, and I noticed that he had his thumb and forefinger at the corners of his mouth, and he would manipulate the corners of his mouth to the configuration of a smile. Noting my curiosity, he said, "We know that a smile has a salubrious effect on one's mood. It is not necessarily the cause for the smile that affects the mood, but the actual muscular activity. I don't have much to smile about today, so I manufacture an artificial smile, because that, too, can lift my mood."

Lest you may think that this is far out, there has been recent evidence to support this concept. One psychiatrist injects a muscle-paralyzing drug into the low forehead muscles of depressed patients, muscles that are used in the formation of a frown. Regardless of how these patients feel, they are unable to frown. This has resulted in significant relief of the depression! So, how we act can affect our mood. Act joyous and you will feel joy.

It is common experience that remembering an unpleasant event can depress one's mood. Conversely, remembering a happy event can lift one's mood. Every person has experienced moments of happiness. If we recall them, and especially if we are able to recreate the happy scene, we can feel happy. I have used this technique with patients, particularly with inducing hypnosis so that they can more easily retrieve happy experiences of the past, even those of childhood years. Patients who suffered with serious illnesses were able to significantly elevate their mood by reliving happy experiences of the past.

Strengthening one's *emunah* (faith) and trust in Hashem is instrumental in generating simchah. People who have firm *emunah* have been able to cope with adversity in a way that it does not crush them. Eliminating the negative effects of adversity allows people to concentrate on the positive, on the feeling that everything they do that is *avodas Hashem* brings them into a closer contact with Hashem.

Emunah is important in achieving simchah not only because it enables a person to cope with adversity, but also because a person who truly believes that Hashem, the Infinite One before Whom supergalaxies are as nothing, has created him for a mission and seeks to develop a relationship with him, will have a feeling of pride and joy. The awareness that every mitzvah one does brings one closer to Hashem endows every mitzvah with simchah.

I believe that self-fulfillment brings about simchah. But what is self-fulfillment?

In the account of creation, there is an important nuance. Every bit of creation, from the tiniest ant to a supergalaxy came into being at the word of G-d. However, when it came to the creation of man, the Torah states, "And G-d said, 'Let us make man'" (*Genesis* 1:26). The obvious question is, to whom does "us" refer? Whose participation was G-d requesting, and why is it only with the creation of man that G-d said, "Let us?"

The Baal Shem Tov explained that Hashem created everything in a state of completion. Animals are born small and need to grow, but they do not have to effect any essential change in themselves. Little alligators become big alligators and little bears become big bears. Even those creatures that undergo a change do not do so volitionally. A caterpillar does not become a butterfly because it thinks butterflies are more beautiful or because flying is a better mode of travel than crawling on the ground. The caterpillar's genes are programmed so that it is transformed into a butterfly whether it wants to or not.

The only exception to this is the human being, who is born essentially an animal, but who must transform himself into Hashem's concept of "man." The definition of "man" is a creature that by his own efforts brings about a change in himself from being essentially an animal that is totally driven by instincts and biological cravings into a spiritual being that is responsible for its actions and has the ability to act ethically and to choose between right and wrong.

Inasmuch as this is Hashem's definition of man, G-d could not create the finished product. A being that was created spiritual would be an angel, not a human being. Hashem's concept of man was that he was to be a being that transformed himself by his own efforts. Therefore, Hashem sought *man's* participation in his formation. Hashem was saying *to man,* "Let us make man. I will give you the potential to become man, but you must develop that potential."

Solomon says that Hashem created man to be *yashar* (just and upright; *Ecclesiastes* 7:29). Man can fulfill himself and hence the purpose for which he was created by becoming *yashar*. The patriarchs — Abraham, Isaac, and Jacob — are our models for this; hence the book of *Genesis*, that describes their lives, is referred to as *Sefer Hayashar* (*Avodah Zarah* 25a). Becoming *yashar* results in simchah, as the psalmist says, *"Le'yishrei lev simchah"* (*Psalms* 97:11), simchah is present when one's heart is *yashar*.

A human being is different from animals not only in being more intelligent, but also in a number of other ways. Among them are: (1) the ability to learn from the history of past generations; (2) the ability to search for truth; (3) the ability to reflect on the purpose and goals of life; (4) the ability to have self-awareness; (5) the ability to volitionally improve oneself; (6) the ability to have perspective, to contemplate the future and to think about consequences resulting from one's actions; (7) the ability to be considerate of others and to be sensitive to their needs; (8) the ability to sacrifice one's comfort and possessions for the welfare of others; (9) the ability to empathize; (10) the ability to make moral and ethical choices in defiance of strong bodily drives and urges; (11) the ability to forgive; (12) the ability to aspire, and (13) the ability to delay gratification. Hashem created man with these abilities, and it is man's duty to execute these abilities, which then makes him the *yashar* that Hashem desired.

It is of interest that the Talmud refers to people who do various things properly as "becoming a partner to Hashem in the work of creation." Becoming the being that Hashem intended affects a human being's fulfillment, and if one fails do so, one is an incomplete or defective being. It stands to reason that a defective being cannot be happy, and that working toward self-fulfillment generates happiness.

This concept is elaborated by R' Samson Raphael Hirsch in his commentary on the verse in *Psalms* (19:9), "The mandates of Hashem are upright, rejoicing the heart."

R' Hirsch notes that the Hebrew word for "mandates," *pikudei*, is related to the word *pikadon*, an object entrusted to someone. Thus, Hashem placed man in *Gan Eden* (Paradise) with the assignment "to work it and to guard it" (*Genesis* 2:15). "All the commandments that regulate our private and public acts are simply directives for the proper discharge of this mandate of 'serving and preserving.' We are told that these *pikudim* are *yesharim*. They are in perfect accord with the nature and calling of the Jewish nation, to whom they were given. Therefore, they are *mesamchei lev*, they rejoice the heart. They give us that joy of life that nothing can ever dim, that satisfaction that comes from a task well done. There can be no substitute for this feeling of quiet joy and serenity, secure in the knowledge that we have done what was expected of us in life, however small or limited the sphere in which our lives are lived. For there is only one true joy, the joy that comes from a life of duty fulfilled, of consecration of all our desires and achievements to the fulfillment of the will of G-d."

There is also a "simchah of anticipation." Of all living things, the human being is the only one who can contemplate the future, and this is indeed a component of intellect, as the Talmud says, "A wise person is one who can foresee the future" (*Tamid* 32a). Even a person who is experiencing distress can look forward to better times. This is one of the ways in which simchah and sadness can coexist. On *Tishah B'Av*, as we mourn the destruction of the Temple and Jerusalem, we do not say the daily prayer of *Tachanun*, which is omitted on festive days. Why? Because the prophet's phrase, "*kara alei moed*" (lit. He proclaimed a set time against me, *Lamentations* 1:15), is also interpreted to mean that Hashem designated *Tishah B'Av* as a *moed*, a day that will be festive when we merit the Ultimate Redemption.

In Psalm 59, after David says, "For I recognize my transgressions, and my sin is before me always. Against You alone I did sin, and that which is evil in Your eyes I did do" (vs. 3-4), he nevertheless continues, "Make me hear joy and gladness, may the bones that You crushed exult" (v. 10) and "Restore to me the joy of Your salvation" (v. 14). Even at moments of profound distress, David anticipates joy.

Tanya addresses the frequently asked question, How can there be a mitzvah to love Hashem? Love is an emotion, and one cannot be ordered to feel something. *Tanya* therefore introduces the concept of "intellectual love." If you know that Hashem deserves to be loved, that, too, is consider *ahavah*, even if one does not feel the emotion. Similarly, there is an "intellectual simchah." If a person realizes that he *should* be feeling joy, as with the fulfillment of mitzvos, then he can be said to have simchah, even though he may not *feel* elated.

On the Passover morning, although I did not feel the elation I should have felt with the fulfillment of mitzvos, I was at least aware that I *should* have felt elated, and that doing mitzvos warrants elation. Thus, I had an "intellectual simchah." Granted, that is not good enough, and I must aim for a feeling of elation with mitzvos, but it was at least a beginning.

We now have several meanings for simchah: (1) the feeling when a personal desire is fulfilled; (2) the simchah of doing a mitzvah; (3) the anticipation of joy in the future; (4) the serenity of accepting Hashem's judgment as just; (5) the feeling that one has grown spiritually; (6) the feeling of self-fulfillment; (7) the feeling that one can just feel (i.e., not having a *lev even*, a heart of stone; (8) the feeling of accomplishment (i.e., process), and (9) "intellectual simchah," the knowledge that one *should be* feeling joy. Although the latter seven may not be what we usually think of as simchah because they are not necessarily joyous in the sense of being merry, they are nevertheless true simchah. With this broad definition, we can see that it is possible for a person to experience *some* form of simchah under all circumstances. Furthermore, if one can develop these other facets of simchah, he may thereby remove the obstacles that prevent him from feeling the actual joy of mitzvos.

7

ALL "SIMCHAS" CAN LEAD TO JOYOUS SIMCHAH

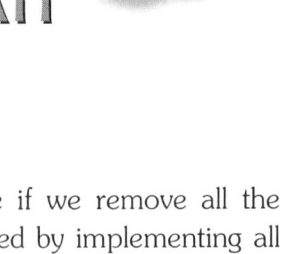

Yes, the simchah of joy is achievable if we remove all the obstacles thereto. This is accomplished by implementing all the other varieties of simchah. It is worthwhile to quote the words of *Nesivas Shalom* (vol.1 p.286).

"Inasmuch as simchah is the key to all the gates of kedushah, it is obviously not its simple meaning, as many assume, which makes it dependent on one's mood, that a person is happy when he has something to be happy about. This cannot be considered to be of lofty spirituality. Rather, simchah is a unique attitude, a path and principle of life that results from a profound understanding, and in all situations and circumstances, regardless of whether one has something to be happy about or not, or whether he has a befitting mood.

"The source of simchah is that a Jew should rejoice in Hashem's conduct with him. This joy should derive from an intense feeling that Hashem is a trustworthy, merciful Father Who is devoted to him, and constantly looks after him to do good for him, and that all His conduct with him is for his benefit, whether or not he understands or feels the good. One should be firm in his belief that everything Hashem does is for the good. This is why this simchah is of such high spirituality.

"With this insight, a Jew can feel simchah, even when in distress, as in the verse (Psalms 91:15), 'I am with him in his anguish.' Whatever occurs to him, even if he falls from his spiritual level and is confused and bewildered, he nevertheless feels the closeness of Hashem, and is not alone in his situation."

R' Hirsch of Rimanov said that when a person awakens in the morning and realizes that Hashem has returned his *neshamah* to him and that he is a newly born person, one should gratefully sing Hashem's praises. R' Hirsch said that he knew a chassid of his master, R' Mendel of Rimanov, who danced joyously when he recited the morning prayer, "My G-d, the *neshamah* You have put within me is pure."

We may find it difficult to identify with people of such lofty spirituality, and we may feel that simchah is beyond our reach. R' Isaac of Zidachow once asked a chassid, "Why are you not happy?" The chassid said, "I have nothing to be happy about." R' Isaac said, "If you needed money but did not have any, you would borrow money from someone, wouldn't you? Well, you need simchah, and if you don't have any of your own, borrow some from someone else."

There is much simchah in Torah literature. We can always borrow some of it.

8
Simchah and the Family

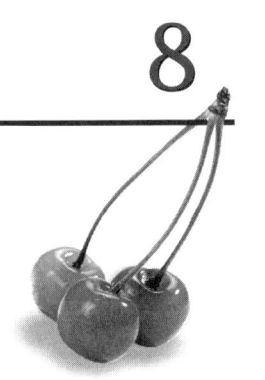

The single greatest responsibility we have is to raise a family that will embrace Yiddishkeit. This is a major challenge in the modern world.

There is no escaping stress, because stress is relative. There is an anecdote about a man who was never able to hold a job, because every job was too stressful. Finally, they got him a job at an orange grove. He was to sit at the bottom of a chute, and when the oranges came down, he was to shift the large oranges to the right and the small oranges to the left. After one day at the job, he quit. "Too much stress," he said. "What kind of stress could you possibly have had?" he was asked. "What do you mean?" he said. "All day, decisions, decisions!"

To this person, deciding whether an orange was large or small was stressful. What an individual considers stress is dependent on one's perceptions. There is stress in everyone's life.

We live in an era where there is little tolerance for stress. Billions of tranquilizers are consumed by people who are perfectly healthy but seek escape from stress. The hedonism in today's society is unprecedented, and many people seek indulgence in pleasure as an escape from the discomfort of the stresses of normal living. Our children are exposed to this ethos and they are at risk of seeking to escape from normal stress rather than to cope effectively with it, and this jeopardizes their Yiddishkeit.

How parents handle stress and discomfort may determine how the children will cope. An attitude of simchah in the home is the greatest source of strength for children.

Understandably, things may occur that preclude, at least temporarily, a feeling of joy. This is when it is essential to enlist simchah, in all its varied facets.

In *It's Not as Tough as You Think* I pointed out many situations that at the moment appeared distressing, but invariably, the unpleasantness faded before long. If children see their parents taking things in stride and retaining an upbeat attitude even in the face of adversity, they are likely to follow suit.

As far as everyone is concerned, things are not the way they are but rather the way one sees them. Much depends on one's perspective. This is masterfully illustrated in the cartoon by Charles Schulz that appears on the following page.

The fact is that it is a bright, sunny day, but if a person mistakes the blackboard for a window, the world seems awfully dark.

Parents may have experienced much stress in their own lives or may have picked up a negative outlook on life from their parents. Regardless, it is within our means to develop a positive attitude. Not only is this the greatest gift we can give our children, but it also assures us of the maximum of *nachas*.

I was privileged to have observed my father, who had no dearth of adversity in his life. Yet, he would enter the room smiling, and exclaim "*Lebedig, kinderlach, lebedig!*" (Be lively,

> "BOY! IS IT EVER DARK OUTSIDE!!"

With permission © October 17, 1948.

my children, be lively!) Everyone in the room, even people older than him, were *kinderlach*, and his cheerful mood was infectious.

Of course, one should not deny reality. Successful coping does not mean that one denies adversity. My *zeide* R' Motele of Hornosteipel, upon hearing that his precious library had been destroyed by fire, was visibly distressed. A few moments later his usual cheerful demeanor returned, and he said to his chassidim, "Why are you not requesting *tikun*?" (Among chassidim, *tikun* consists of drinking a *L'chaim* on appropriate occasions.) The chassidim asked, "Why would we want *tikun* now?" *Zeide* R' Motele said, "The Talmud says that one must praise Hashem with simchah for bad happenings just as for good happenings. If I had won a sweepstakes, would you not have requested *tikun*? Then you should do so now."

The chassidim asked, "But we saw that the Rebbe was deeply grieved by the news of the fire." "Of course," *Zeide* R' Motele said. "When Hashem causes a misfortune to happen, one must feel the pain. But after that, one must accept it as being good, because nothing that is truly bad emanates from Hashem."

Developing a callous indifference to adversity is a denial of reality, and such denial does not prepare one for dealing effectively with reality. When we are hurt, our children should see that we indeed feel the distress, but that we can rise above it and continue with a positive attitude toward life.

A healthy attitude of simchah, as variously defined above, enables the family to share with and support one another, so that the joy of happy occasions is maximized and the distress of unhappy occurrences is contained.

It is necessary to counteract the erroneous cultural concept that "pursuit of pleasure" constitutes "pursuit of happiness." Parents should have discussions with their children about the real meaning of enduring happiness. However, discussions alone are insufficient. Children should see their parents pursuing simchah in all its aspects.

We cannot give our children happiness. We *can* provide them with the tools wherewith they can forge their own happiness. These are the tools of simchah.

Parents should have much simchah in the knowledge that they are raising their children to be upright, G-d-fearing people. They are thereby performing a mitzvah of immeasurable importance, and this should give them simchah.

Not always do the parents see their children fulfill their aspirations. Unfortunately some children may stray from the path of their parental instructions. As distressing as this may be, the parents should not lose heart.

Hashem said, "I love Abraham because he will instruct his children and his household after him that they keep the way of Hashem, doing charity and justice" (*Genesis* 18:19). Only one of Abraham's seven children followed in his footsteps, yet Hashem loved him because he tried. Similarly, in our prayers we invoke the merits of Isaac, only one of whose sons was righteous. Yet, this does not detract from Isaac's greatness, because he tried.

Parents who have the proper intentions and make every effort to raise their children properly should feel a simchah for their efforts.

8: Simchah and the Family / 53

The following chapters will deal with the special times during a Jew's life span. We will learn why we should and how we can have simchah in our lives. By living each day to its fullest and by fulfilling the mitzvos with simchah we can infuse our lives and our homes with this precious multifaceted entity. The end result will be a greater capacity to serve our Father, our King to the best of our ability.

9

SHABBOS — THE HOLINESS OF TIME

We exist in time and in space. Our space is expandable. We can acquire more space by purchasing it or by seizing it. Our time is not expandable. If we have genes of longevity, we may live to a ripe old age, but we cannot acquire more time, either by money or by force, the way we can acquire more space. Logic tells us that time should be the more valuable of the two, yet people protect their space while they often waste time.

Yiddishkeit values time above space. The first instance of *kedushah* (holiness) in the Torah is not of space. At creation, Hashem's Presence was the same everywhere. It was not until the Israelites erred with the worship of the Golden Calf that Hashem commanded the construction of the *Mishkan* (Tabernacle), and the Immanent Presence of Hashem was found in a circumscribed space. But at the very end of creation, time was hallowed. "And Hashem blessed the seventh day and sanctified it" (*Genesis* 2:3).

The sanctity of time permeates Yiddishkeit. In addition to Shabbos, the festivals are holy: "He sanctifies Israel and the *zemanim* (festivals, lit. "times"). Our daily prayers are organized according to time: *Shacharis* in the morning, *Minchah* in the afternoon, *Maariv* in the evening. Every four weeks we recite a prayer to inaugurate and bless the coming month. We celebrate the new month with *Hallel*, singing the praises of Hashem in gratitude just as we do for His great wonders, to show our appreciation of time.

"They shall rejoice in Your kingship, those who observe Shabbos and call it a delight. The people who sanctify Shabbos — they will be satisfied and delighted from Your goodness" (Shabbos prayers). Yiddishkeit values time and finds simchah in time. How different from the secular world that develops and uses time-saving devices, as if they valued time, and then squanders the saved time on inane pastimes. How paradoxical that people can seek happiness in "fun," by killing time! It is noteworthy that there is no word in Hebrew for fun, because the concept of fun — purposeless activity (e.g., Why? For the fun of it) — is alien to Yiddishkeit. One cannot attain happiness by destroying the most valuable commodity that a human being has: *time*.

"They shall rejoice in Your kingship, those who observe Shabbos and call it a delight." Shabbos is an appreciation of time and a key to simchah.

The secular world, too, has a day of rest. The Midrash states that when Moses was in the good graces of Pharaoh, he suggested that the Israelite slaves be given a day of rest so that they could do their work better for the next six days. This kind of rest day, intended to restore one's energies so that one can be more productive in the following days, makes the day of rest subordinate to the workweek. This is not Shabbos. Hashem's "resting" on the seventh day was not because He was exhausted. It was because creation had come to a completion in six days, but was yet without a goal and purpose. The seventh day was "sanctified and blessed" by Hashem as being the goal of creation. The workweek is subordinate to Shabbos.

The Torah states that man was the last of Hashem's creations, and as we have seen, man was created in an incomplete state and assigned the task of developing himself into the Divine concept of what *man* should be. He was given the charge to subdue and dominate the land. However, he was to do this as *man*, not like the wild beasts that dominate the jungle. Six days are to dominate the world, and the seventh day is for man to become master over himself. It is noteworthy that Adam was not given fire until after he had experienced Shabbos (which is why we recite the blessing for fire at *Havdalah* at night when Shabbos departs). Man could not be trusted with the potentially destructive power of fire until he was able to become spiritual and achieve control over himself.

That is the purpose of Shabbos, a blessed and holy day on which a person can elevate oneself spiritually and achieve self-fulfillment. Inasmuch as self-fulfillment is a requisite for simchah, Shabbos is a day of simchah.

Hashem said to Moses, "I have a unique gift in My treasury that I wish to give to the Children of Israel. Its name is Shabbos. Inform them of this" (*Shabbos* 10a). Shabbos is indeed a unique Divine gift.

It is of interest that the mitzvah of Shabbos was not given at Sinai, but a bit earlier at Marah (*Sanhedrin* 56b). This is because Shabbos is a *prerequisite* to the acceptance of Torah.

The desire for comfort and pleasure is innate in humans. Yet we see that people overcome the desire to remain in the comfort of a warm bed and arise on a cold winter day, braving the elements to go to work or to school. They are motivated to do so by their goal to earn money or gain an education, and it is the pursuit of a goal that causes them to defy the bodily desire for warmth and comfort. Without a goal in life, people would not undergo any discomfort.

Most of our daily activities are directed to intermediate goals. We drive the car to the gas station with the goal to obtain fuel, but this is obviously not an ultimate goal. If we had nowhere to go with the car, obtaining fuel would be meaningless. Our next goal is to drive to work or to school, but if work and school were not goal directed, they, too, would have little meaning. Intermediate goals have meaning only if they lead to an ultimate goal.

The secular world appears to operate on the premise that one's ultimate goal is attaining the maximum of pleasure available to man. If, however, experiencing pleasure is a legitimate ultimate goal, most of humanity is wasting a great deal of energy and subjecting itself to unnecessary distress, and society's dictates are misguided. This goal is more readily achieved by use of euphoriant chemicals, which, indeed, is the goal of the drug addict. The universal disapproval of drug addiction indicates that society does not accept pleasure as a legitimate ultimate goal. Rather, society believes that accomplishing something worthwhile in the world is a legitimate ultimate goal.

Furthermore, if being content is the goal of human life, then the human brain is a gross mistake. Cows in the pasture are much more content than humans. As Solomon says (*Ecclesiastes* 1:18), "As one increases intelligence, one increases pain." (The colloquialism for this is, "Ignorance is bliss.") The offices of psychotherapists are populated by people who suffer from anxiety and emotional disorders that are generated by their intellect. Clearly, the human mind was not intended for the pursuit of pleasure as an ultimate goal.

The Steipler Gaon says that if you see a child wearing a jacket whose sleeves extend far beyond his arms, trousers that drag behind him, and a hat that comes down below his nose, you know that these are not his clothes. He has obviously put on his father's clothes. Similarly, when you see what the human mind is capable of, it is clearly not designed for the pursuit of pleasure or contentment. It is grossly oversized for that.

It is difficult to conceive of an ultimate goal and purpose to the life of an individual if the entire universe is purposeless. A universe that was created can have a purpose, having been brought into existence by a Creator. A universe that happened to accidentally come about as a result of a freak accident involving primordial energy and matter and was not designed for any purpose is, therefore, purposeless.

There is a story of two vagrants who were arrested for loitering. The judge asked the first vagrant, "What were you doing when the officer arrested you?" "Nothing," the vagrant answered. The judge then turned to the second vagrant, "And what were you doing when you were arrested?" The man pointed toward his buddy. "I was helping him," he said. It is obvious that if one is helping someone who is doing nothing, one is likewise doing nothing.

Unless there is an ultimate purpose to the universe, all human activities, regardless of how praiseworthy they may be, are only a series of intermediate goals, reminiscent of "the bridge that goes nowhere." In a purposeless world, a Torah would be nothing more than a set of rules for social conduct, subject to change at the whim of society. There would be no absolute good and bad.

The giving of the Torah had to be preceded by Shabbos, which is a testimony to creation. "In six days, G-d created the heaven and the earth, and He rested on the seventh day." It is Shabbos that gives meaning to life.

Shabbos is referred to as *mei'ein olam haba*, akin to the bliss of Paradise. Shabbos should be akin to the Shabbos on which Hashem rested from creation. The whole world was complete, and this is how our Shabbos should be

The mitzvah of Shabbos is bipartite, consisting of a negative commandment, the prohibition of work, and a positive commandment, to sanctify the day. The Torah says that on the seventh day, *shavas vayinafash*. *Shavas* means that G-d abstained from creation, and *vayinafash* means that G-d instilled a *nefesh* into Shabbos. Just as a person has a body and a spirit, so does Shabbos have a "body" — the restriction of work — and a spirit — a *nefesh* and *neshamah*. Abstinence from work is only half of the mitzvah. The other half is making Shabbos into a day of *neshamah*.

Just as Shabbos cannot be sanctified if one works, neither can it be properly sanctified if one carries thoughts and concerns of the workweek into Shabbos. While the latter is not considered a frank violation of the prohibition of work, it is an obstacle toward the sanctification of Shabbos. On the verse, "Six days shall you labor and do all your work" (*Exodus* 20:9), Rashi comments that at the end of the sixth day, one should consider all one's work as having been completed. There are to be no carryovers from the work-week into Shabbos. With the advent of Shabbos, one does not owe any money nor is one owed any money. There are no delays in delivery of merchandise and no unfulfilled orders. One does not think about one's investments. All repairs on the house have been made. There is absolutely nothing that should distract a person from the spirituality of Shabbos. Everything pertaining to the work-week has been completed, and the forgiveness of sins has removed another source of worry. With all the burdens of the past removed, one is free to contemplate spirituality and holiness.

A case in point.

At 45, Nathan had developed a very successful insurance firm, in which he had worked 12 to 14 hours a day. He then suffered a massive heart attack and, after two months, was told by his doctor to limit his presence at the office to two hours a day. After several weeks, Nathan was very dissatisfied with this restriction, but his wife, Leah, made him follow the doctor's orders.

Nathan then received a handsome offer to buy out his firm. He jumped at the opportunity, sold the business, and convinced Leah that they should sell their spacious home and move to a condominium in Florida.

The dream of blissful retirement was short lived. Nathan was a type-A personality, accustomed to operating under pressure. He had never developed any way of using leisure time except as a brief respite from work, to recharge his batteries for the next workday. Most of the people in the condominium complex were older retirees, and Nathan did not feel he had much in common with them. Leah made herself a flower garden which she carefully cultivated, and joined the local congregation sisterhood. Nathan had no patience for the men's club. Leisure time weighed heavily on his hands and he became depressed.

Proper observance of Shabbos might have prevented Nathan's depression. He would have learned how to put leisure time to constructive use.

At the Friday-night meal, my mother would serve *ferfel*, which is related to the Yiddish word *ferfallen*, bygone, over and done with. As she brought the *ferfel* to the table, she would say, "Whatever was until now is *ferfallen*." Shabbos eliminates the accumulated concerns of the past.

The proper observance of Shabbos requires that one's conduct should be different than that of the weekdays. We should walk leisurely, not with the haste and frenzy of the workweek. And our speech on Shabbos should not be like that of the weekday.

Speech, even during the week, must follow halachah. *Lashon hara* (defamatory speech) must be scrupulously avoided. *Rechilus* (carrying tales) is forbidden. One may not use *nivul peh* (indecent language). Not only is frank lying forbidden (*lo teshakru*, Leviticus 19:11), but one must also avoid anything that could lead to an untruth (*mid'var shekker tirchak*; Exodus 23:7). *Devarim beteilim* (idle talk) is likewise unacceptable (*Yoma* 19b).

Given these guidelines, which are halachically mandatory and not merely optional piety, our speech during the weekdays should be spiritual in nature. The requirement that our speech on Shabbos be different than that of the week elevates it even further, essentially restricting speech on Shabbos to words of Torah teachings and praises of Hashem. Indeed, there are people who do not converse at all on Shabbos, other than for Torah study and prayer. According to the halachos of speech as described by the Chafetz Chaim, our speech during the weekdays must be *kodesh* (sanctified). It follows that on Shabbos, our speech must be *kodesh kadashim*, of the highest sanctity and spiritual level.

Many people usher in Shabbos with the reading of *Song of Songs*, Solomon's parable depicting the passionate longing of Israel and Hashem to be in an intimate bond. In the services, Shabbos is welcomed as a queen in the *Lechah Dodi* hymn, where Israel says to Hashem, "Come, my Beloved, toward the bride. Let us greet the Shabbos."

On Friday night, the challah is covered during *Kiddush*, the prayer testifying to the six days of creation and that Hashem rested on the seventh day. The reason for covering the challah is that according to halachah, the *berachah* (blessing) for bread takes precedence to the *berachah* for wine. Inasmuch as the *Kiddush* is recited over wine, the challah is covered to prevent its being humiliated when the *berachah* for wine is recited first. Obviously, the inanimate challah cannot experience humiliation. The practice of covering the challah is symbolic, to impress upon us how exquisitely sensitive we must be to other people's feelings. This sensitivity should characterize our interpersonal relationships, especially on Shabbos.

Of all the activities that are forbidden on Shabbos that are derived by Talmudic exegesis, the Torah singles out one: "You shall not kindle a flame in all your dwellings" (*Exodus* 35:3). Rabbi Chaim of Czernovitz (*Siduro shel Shabbos*) explains that in addition to being a forbidden type of work, making a fire also refers to the flame of rage. Inasmuch as rage is forbidden at any time, the special precaution means that we must make extra effort to avoid anger on Shabbos.

Hagaon Harav Avraham Pam cites the Midrash that Adam sinned late on Friday, and that the day of Shabbos pleaded that he not be punished then. "You said that You blessed the seventh day and sanctified it. Is it a blessing and sanctity that man should be punished on my day?" (*Yalkut Shimoni*). Although it is forbidden to cause another person any anguish during the week, it is an even greater sin to do so on Shabbos. The day of Shabbos may complain, "Is this my sanctity and blessing?"

Shabbos, as a day blessed by Hashem, is propitious for blessings. It is customary that before *Kiddush* on Friday night, the father blesses the children. How wonderful it would be if children would realize that their blessing comes from their parents, and for parents to realize that they should relate to the children in a way that they would be the conduit for Hashem's blessing to the children.

The attractiveness and sweetness of Shabbos is in the fulfillment of the halachos and customs that elevate Shabbos to the zenith of spirituality. This is indeed a state of ecstasy that is *mei'ein olam haba*, akin to the bliss of Paradise. For some *tzaddikim*, Shabbos surpassed *olam haba*. Rabbi Baruch of Medzhibozh said, "I would exchange ten *olam habas* for one Shabbos." We may not be able to achieve a Shabbos experience like Rabbi Baruch, but we must learn to observe Shabbos in a manner that it is at least *mei'ein olam haba,* just a taste of Paradise.

Celebrating Shabbos with three meals is of such great merit that the Talmud says, "Whoever observes the three meals of Shabbos is spared from three forms of punishment: from the anguish prior to the coming of *Mashiach,* from the judgment of *Gehinnom,* and from the battle of *Gog and Magog.* Furthermore, his prayers are answered" (*Shabbos* 118a). Of course, this refers to partaking of the three meals with the appropriate *kavannah* (intent), *kedushah,* and *divrei Torah.*

Shabbos afternoon, usually after *Minchah,* there is the third meal, usually a token meal, consisting of challah and fish. (Of course, one may serve a full meal if one wishes.)

Among chassidim, this third meal, *seudah shelishis,* is eaten in the gathering darkness. According to kabbalah, this time is the zenith of Shabbos, and is a specially propitious time. Sitting in the dark, there are no distractions, and it is conducive to meditation.

This meal is often referred to as *shalosh seudos,* which means "three meals." *Divrei Emes* explains that the first two meals of Shabbos — Friday night and Shabbos morning after *davening* — are full meals that one eats when hungry. There is no indication that one partakes primarily to fulfill the mitzvah. However, the third meal, a token meal eaten when one is not hungry, is obviously to fulfill the mitzvah of three meals on Shabbos. This indicates that the first two meals were also in honor of Shabbos. Therefore, it is *shalosh seudos,* because it encompasses all three meals. Chassidic rebbes usually give a discourse on *chassidus* at *shalosh seudos.*

Tradition has transmitted to us many tasty foods for Shabbos and the Festivals. We indeed partake of them, but we should not lose sight of their purpose. Having appeased the body with these delicious foods, we should dedicate ourselves to the spiritual aspects of Shabbos and the Festivals.

When Shabbos comes to a close, the prospect of leaving this spiritual experience and returning to the workweek with all its stresses and drudgery can be depressing. This transition is mitigated by the Shabbos-night meal, the *Melaveh Malkah.*

In contrast to the delicacies of the Shabbos meals, the menu of the *Melaveh Malkah* meal Shabbos night is generally rather sparse. *Melaveh Malkah* means "escorting the queen," referring to parting with "Queen Shabbos." The regular menu may be herring, borscht, and potatoes. The potatoes are cooked especially for the *Melaveh Malkah* to demonstrate that we refrained from cooking on Shabbos because the Torah forbade it, and that when Shabbos was over, we are permitted to cook once again. Yet, this simple meal was actually the most enjoyable one for me, because it was customary to relate stories about our *tzaddikim*, stories that fascinated me, some of which I recorded in *Not Just Stories*.

Stories are a powerful method of communication. The chassidic master, R' Yisroel of Rizhin, said, "When the Baal Shem Tov sought Divine intervention to save the Jews from misfortune, he would seclude himself in the forest, light a fire, and say a special prayer.

"When his successor, my great-grandfather, the Maggid of Mezeritch, wished to intercede for his people, he would go to the same place in the forest and say, 'Master of the Universe! I do not know how to light the fire, but I can still say the prayer,' and with that he evoked Divine mercy.

"Later, R' Moshe Leib of Sasov would go to the place in the forest and say, 'I do not know how to light the fire and I do not know the prayer. Master of the Universe! Have compassion upon us by the merits of the *tzaddikim* who prayed to You here.'"

R' Yisroel would put his head in his hands and say, "Master of the Universe! I do not know how to light the fire, I do not know the prayer, and I do not even find the place in the forest. All I know is the story about how these *tzaddikim* interceded for their people, and this must be sufficient."

Stories are the vehicle that can move metaphor and images into experience. Stories can communicate what is generally invisible and inexpressible. Of all the devices available to us, stories are the surest way of touching the human spirit. And *Melaveh Malkah* was rich in stories. My personal opinion is that the sages instituted *Melaveh Malkah* to dispel the post-Shabbos blues.

The Gaon of Vilna was extremely diligent in observing *Melaveh Malkah*. It is related that the Gaon's wife frequently fasted, and that the Gaon said to her, "All your fasts do not add up to the merit of a single *Melaveh Malkah.*"

One Shabbos night the Gaon was ill and could not eat anything. He slept for a few hours and when he awoke and saw that it was before dawn, he quickly ate a small piece of challah for *Melaveh Malkah.*

The *Melaveh Malkah* is referred to as the "feast of King David." The reason for this is based on the Midrash that David asked G-d to reveal to him when he would die. G-d said that this is never revealed to a person, but told him that he would die on Shabbos. Therefore, when Shabbos passed and David was alive, he made a feast to celebrate his reprieve for at least one more week of life"

In the *zemiros* (songs) of the *Melaveh Malkah,* we say, "David, king of Israel, lives and exists," thereby expressing our belief in the reestablishment of the royal lineage of David with the Ultimate Redemption. We also say, *Siman tov u'mazal tov,* good omens and good fortune shall come to us and to all of Israel.

The *zemiros* also feature the prophet Elijah. The Talmud says that Elijah, who will herald the Ultimate Redemption, will not do so on Erev Shabbos or on Erev Yom Tov, so that the celebration of Shabbos and Yom Tov should not be disrupted. Therefore, when Shabbos passes, we sing about Elijah, inviting him to bring us the good tidings of the Redemption.

As we noted, David's life was one of uninterrupted suffering, yet, even in his moments of anguish, David could say, "Return to me the joy of Your salvation" (*Psalms* 51:14), never abandoning hope for happiness. We begin the new week with the inspiration of David, that simchah is always within reach. Elijah is not only the personification of immortality, but is also the harbinger of the Ultimate Redemption. Countless times in Jewish history, Elijah has appeared in human form to comfort the suffering.

King David, the prophet Elijah, and stories of *tzaddikim* — *Melaveh Malkah* is indeed a potent antidepressant. The entire Shabbos is thus a lesson in achieving simchah.

I experienced the power of the simchah of Shabbos on my first visit to Israel. In keeping with halachah, I wept and tore my garment at the Western Wall just as one does on the loss of a loved one. On Friday night, I joined in a joyous dance at the Western Wall as we sang *Lechah Dodi*, A conflict? No, I wept in space and rejoiced in time.

It is customary, when praying for a sick person on Shabbos, to say "*Shabbos he melizok, u'refuah kerovah lavo*" (though Shabbos prohibits us from crying out, may a recover come speedily).

The *tzaddik*, R' Hillel of Paritsch, once visited a town where a number of Jews kept their shops open on Shabbos. R' Hillel called them together and impressed upon them the overriding importance of observing Shabbos. The shopkeepers agreed, on the condition that the rich man who owned the largest store would close his store on Shabbos, because otherwise they could not compete with him. R' Hillel sent for this wealthy man, but he refused to come. A second messenger was sent, but was also turned away.

Shabbos morning, the wealthy man began having severe abdominal pain, which grew worse from hour to hour. His wife concluded that this occurred because he had offended the *tzaddik*, and pleaded with R' Hillel that he should forgive her husband and pray for him, but R' Hillel remained silent. The chassidim who were with him said, "Rebbe, can't you just say, '*Shabbos he melizok, u'refuah kerovah lavo*' ?" but R' Hillel remained silent.

Shabbos night, at *Melaveh Malkah*, the wife again came, pleading tearfully that R' Hillel pray for her husband. R' Hillel said, "*Shabbos he melizok, u'refuah kerovah lavo*. This can be translated as 'If Shabbos will refrain from crying out, recovery will come speedily.' Shabbos has been crying out that this person is desecrating it. If he gives his solemn promise that he will close his store on Shabbos, he will recover."

The chassidim hurried to the man's bedside and told him what the *tzaddik* said. The man promptly promised to observe Shabbos, and soon recovered.

10

TEFILLAH (PRAYER)

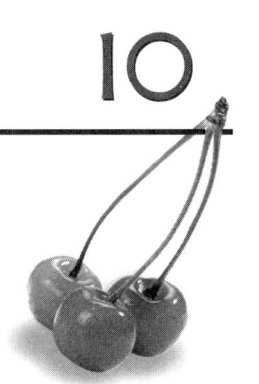

It has been said that Torah is Hashem speaking to man, and *tefillah* (prayer) is man speaking to Hashem. In *tefillah*, we ask Hashem for many of our needs. If we understand that simchah is one of our needs, we should pray for simchah. David frequently prayed for simchah, as we have seen, "Return to me the joy of Your salvation" (*Psalms* 51:14).

There are several origins for the word *tefillah*. One meaning is "bonding" (Rashi, *Genesis* 30:8). Prayer is a way in which man binds oneself to Hashem. Inasmuch as this is an ultimate goal for man, *tefillah* is of unparalleled importance in Yiddishkeit. Working toward this goal with *tefillah* and because it is self-fulfilling, is adequate reason for simchah. For a person to bond with Hashem, the barriers that preclude such bonding must be eliminated.

Unfortunately, prayer has not received its due. The Talmud says, "Do not make your prayer a set routine, but rather a compassion and supplication before Hashem" (*Ethics of the Fathers* 2:18). Far too often, prayer is not only routinized, but is also said in great haste, so that one can attend to "more important things" the rest of the day. We would hardly consider a small portion of appetizer as constituting a meal. Neither should we consider a hurried prayer as adequate.

In the *Shema* we say, "And you shall love Hashem, your G-d, with all your heart, with all your soul, and with all your might" (*Deuteronomy* 6:5). As we have noted, several commentaries ask, "How can you legislate love? Love is an emotion. It is either there or not there. Can you order someone to love?"

The answer is that within each person, there is an innate, inherent love for Hashem that is a bequest from the patriarch Abraham. It is concealed within us, clouded by our love for mundane things that are anathema to the *neshamah*. If we rid ourselves of the love for things restricted by Torah, and overcome our desire to indulge in physicality, the innate love for Hashem will emerge. This theme is especially developed in *Tanya*.

In trying to bond with Hashem, we are inviting Him to be with us. The Maggid of Dubnow explains that if someone invited distinguished guests into his home, he would clean the house and make certain that there was nothing that would be offensive to his guests. Similarly, the bonding with Hashem cannot occur if there are feelings and behavior that are inimical to Hashem.

In one of his inimitable parables, the Maggid tells of a peasant who came to a store of fine clothing and asked for a suit. The salesperson estimated his size and gave him a suit that was appropriate for him. The peasant put on the suit on top of the coarse clothing he was wearing and complained that the suit did not fit. "You fool!" the salesperson berated him. "You must first take off the coarse garments you are wearing, and then the suit will fit you perfectly." That is how it is with the bonding to Hashem. It cannot fit unless we divest ourselves of the coarse love we harbor for many earthly pleasures.

The essence of prayer was stated by King David: "One thing I asked of Hashem, that I shall seek — that I dwell in the House of Hashem all the days of my life, to behold the sweetness of Hashem and to contemplate in His Sanctuary" (*Psalms* 27:4). "One thing I asked" means that this is the *entire* focus of prayer, and all aspects of prayer must be directed toward the goal "that I dwell in the House of Hashem all the days of my life."

There is another answer to the question: How can you legislate love? Rambam (*Yesodei HaTorah* 2:2) states: "What is the way to achieve love of Hashem? If a person will meditate on His great and marvelous works and see from them His wisdom that is beyond measure and infinite, one will promptly love, praise, and exalt Hashem, and have an intense desire to know Him." At first glance, this does not appear to answer the question. Awareness of the grandeur of nature and Hashem's infinite wisdom and power may result in exaltation and adoration, but how does it produce love?

The *peirush* (commentary) on Rambam says that Rambam is redefining the word *ahavah*, generally translated as "love." The *ahavah* with which we are most familiar is that between two people — parent and child, husband and wife. This *ahavah* is generally contingent on the benefits one derives from the relationship. Rambam says that there is a second type of *ahavah*, which, rather than love, is a desire to be in the close presence of someone, in an intimate relationship, as a result of the adoration of someone.

We may get an inkling of this desire for a close presence by observing the "hero worship" that a child may have for a prominent sports figure. Such a child will collect pictures of his hero, and he is thrilled to get his autograph. He may mimic his hero's actions, and if the child is asked, "If you had just one wish, what would it be?" the child may well answer "I'd just like to get to know X." To be close to his hero may be the child's most fervent desire.

It is the intense desire to be near Hashem, in an intimate relationship with Him, that Rambam defines as *ahavah*. Rambam has good reason for this concept. Moses says, "(I instruct you) to love Hashem, to hearken to His voice, and *to cleave to Him.*" Moses is essentially defining *ahavah* as "cleaving unto Hashem."

In order to achieve the adoration of Hashem that will produce this type of *ahavah*, Rambam says that one must reflect on His marvelous works. This theme is stated in *Tehillim* (*Psalms* 104) where King David extols the wondrous and beautiful world, exclaiming, "How abundant are Your works, Hashem. With wisdom You have made them all. The world is full of Your acquisitions," and "When I see Your heavens, the work of Your fingers, the moon and the stars that You have set in place" (*Yesodei Hatorah* 8:4).

If only one understood the incomparable marvel of the human body! If all the computers in the world were combined, they would be dwarfed by the relatively small organ, the human brain, which has perhaps *100 billion* parts (cells) that are multiply and complexly interconnected. My professor of neurophysiology said that from the time a pitcher throws the baseball until the batter swings, hundreds of thousands of messages are transmitted through the central nervous system.

A physician said, "I was looking through a microscope at a fertilized ovum, and I realized that from now on, all that would be added to it would be nutrient chemicals, and from these this tiny, single cell would fashion a human being, I knew then that there is a G-d."

It was David's awareness of the awesome grandeur of Hashem's works that led him to say, "My soul thirsts for You; my flesh pines for You" (*Psalms* 63:2). This is what Rambam defines as *ahavah*, and it is within our means to achieve this. This is the bonding of *tefillah*. The knowledge that we are bonding with Hashem is reason for joy.

Tefillah is a vital need, and just as we pray to Hashem for all other needs, we should pray to Him for *tefillah*. In other words, we should pray for the ability to pray. There is indeed a "Prayer before Prayer" that can be found in some of the larger *siddurim*, and was composed by R' Elimelech of Lizhensk.

In this prayer, R' Elimelech pleads with Hashem for relief from the *yetzer hara*, which interferes with our prayer, even at a time when we are pleading for our very lives. Is it conceivable that a person who was begging a judge or a king to spare his life would harbor any extraneous thoughts?

When a tightrope walker came to a town and announced his performance, a chassidic rebbe took a number of his followers to watch this performance. Afterward he said to them, "The only way that the tightrope walker could keep his balance was because he was completely focused on what he was doing. Had any extraneous thoughts distracted him for even a second, he would have fallen to his death. He could not even think about the money he would get for this stunt. That is the attitude you should have when you pray or do a mitzvah. You should be so completely focused on what you are doing that it would be impossible for any alien thought to enter your mind."

It is of great interest that R' Elimelech closes his prayer with a plea to Hashem to spare him from envy or from dislike of any person. "May I always see the merits in others, and not their shortcomings." A benign and favorable attitude toward others is necessary for proper *tefillah*. Seeing faults in other people or disliking them is a barrier to bonding with Hashem. In some *siddurim*, there is a verse preceding the service, "I hereby accept upon myself the mitzvah of 'Love your fellow as you do yourself.'" Of course, this should be a true commitment, not just lip service.

Do we really know what to pray for? The *tzaddik* of Sanz used to relate the following parable before Rosh Hashanah.

A prince once committed a transgression for which he was punished by being exiled to a far corner of his father's empire. Having never learned how to do anything with his hands, he did not have a way to earn a livelihood. Inasmuch as no skill was required to watch a herd of sheep, he hired himself out as a shepherd. Sitting in the heat of the sun, he was very uncomfortable. He noticed that other shepherds built themselves little thatched huts for shade, but every time he tried to build a hut, it collapsed.

One day he heard that there was to be a royal parade. The custom was that people would write petitions and throw them toward the royal coach, and the king would grant the requests of those petitions that fell into the coach. The shepherd wrote a petition that he would like to have a hut to provide shade from the sun. This petition landed in the coach, and when the king recognized his son's handwriting, he wept. "How low my son has fallen. He has resigned himself to being a shepherd, and aspires only to a hut. He could have requested to be taken back to the palace, where he would live the luxurious life of a prince!"

The *tzaddik* of Sanz would weep as he related this parable. "Rosh Hashanah is approaching, and it is a most propitious time to bring our requests before Hashem. We should ask for the Redemption, to be returned to the Holy Land where we would live in intimate contact with Hashem. Instead, like the prince, we have resigned ourselves to living in exile, and all we ask for is petty things to make our life in exile more comfortable. How painful this must be for Hashem, that His children have forgotten that they are princes!"

The ideal prayer is that of David, to be taken into the immanent presence of Hashem. But, the Amidah (*Shemoneh Esrei* Prayer) does indeed include personal requests, for wisdom, forgiveness, good health, and *parnassah* (livelihood). In what way is this the ideal prayer? The answer is that we are not angels. In order for us to desire bonding with Hashem, we must realize that we are totally dependent upon Him. The personal requests are to make us aware of our absolute dependence on Hashem.

The *Zohar* makes a cryptic statement: "Israel gives *parnassah* to their Heavenly Father" (III 7:2). The commentaries explain that Hashem's desire is to bestow His infinite kindness on Israel. "The cow's desire to nurse her calf is greater than the calf's desire to be fed" (*Pesachim* 112a). However, inasmuch as Hashem conducts the world within the parameters of justice, He cannot give of His kindness when people are not deserving of it. When we pray and plead to Hashem as a child to his father, it is within justice for a father to have mercy on his child, even if the child has not been behaving properly. Therefore, when we pray sincerely, we give Hashem the opportunity to give of His kindness to us. As it were, we are providing for Hashem. How joyous would you feel if you were privileged to give a gift to a king, and he thanked you for it? Our prayer is a gift to Hashem, and inasmuch as Hashem receives all our prayers, we should have simchah in praying.

Another explanation is that we are told that when Jews suffer, Hashem participates in their suffering, as the Psalmist says (91:15), "I am with him in his anguish." The Talmud frequently refers to this phenomenon (e.g., *Toras Kohanim, Acharei* 13). If a person who is suffering can have the *kavannah* that he is praying for relief so that Hashem is relieved of His suffering, this too is providing for Hashem.

Commentaries address the question: In what way is prayer effective? Can we cause Hashem to change His mind and give us what we ask for if He had not preordained it? In light of what was just said, we can answer this question. A person who prays properly undergoes spiritual growth, and becomes more deserving after prayer than before prayer. It is not that Hashem changes His mind, but that the person changes for the better.

But in what way is the prayer for others effective? If one prays for the health of a sick person, the latter is not undergoing spiritual growth when someone else prays for him.

The commentaries cite Hashem's statement to Moses when He threatened to punish Israel for worshipping the Golden Calf. Hashem said, "And now, desist from Me. Let My anger flare up against them" (*Exodus* 32:10). Hashem was telling Moses that the fate of Israel was in his hands, and that if he prayed for them, they would be forgiven. In other words, the Divine will was originally that if Moses would pray for them, Hashem would forgive them. Hashem did not change His mind.

I learned something about prayer at the Western Wall. I was reciting *Tehillim*, when I saw a blind man being led to the Wall. He felt the Wall with his fingers, kissed it gently, and began a conversation with Hashem. Abruptly he paused and said, "Oh, I already told You that yesterday." I realized that he was certain that Hashem had heard him the previous day.

The Talmud says that one should pray with a solemn attitude (*Berachos* 30b), but also states that one should pray amid the feeling of joy from a mitzvah (ibid. 31a). It would seem that solemnity and joy cannot coexist simultaneously. The fact is that they can, as David says, "Rejoice with trembling" (*Psalms* 2:11). The following anecdote illustrates this.

A chassid presented a petition to R' Shneur Zalman of Liadi. The rebbe studied the petition, then said, "It seems that you have given much thought to your needs. Have you also given much thought to why you are needed?" The chassid trembled with this reprimand, but was also thrilled to realize that indeed, he was needed, and that there is a specific purpose in the world that he must fulfill. His existence was not an accident. He was important, and Hashem had a mission for him, one that only he could fulfill. This was most edifying. The chassid was at once trembling but joyous.

This attitude is reflected in the prayer, *Avinu Malkeinu*, Our Father, Our King. We relate to Hashem with the love and familiarity of a child to a father, and also with the awe and reverence of a subject for his king. Our awareness that we are beloved children to Hashem as well as His subjects is certainly reason for simchah.

True *tefillah* is more than the recitation of the prayers in the *siddur*. There should be an intense desire to relate to Hashem.

At a Shabbaton, a woman approached me and said, "I was very envious of you today. I walked by the shul and I saw you praying. I so wanted to pray, but I know nothing about prayer."

I said to her, "Hashem knows what is within our hearts. I suspect that when Hashem sees me enter the shul, He says, 'What does he want this time? He is always asking for something. "Give me this," or "I need that." ' When Hashem saw you standing outside the shul, wanting to pray, He read the thoughts in your heart and said, 'There is my child. She wants to reach Me, but does not know how.' I suspect that your unspoken prayer was dearer to Hashem than my recitation of the formal prayers."

There are many anecdotes about the effectiveness of heartfelt prayers. R' David of Mikalyav took one of his disciples with him to spend Yom Kippur with his master, R' Pinchas of Koretz. They ate and drank in preparation for the fast day, and the disciple fell into a deep sleep, waking up only toward the end of Yom Kippur when the people were praying *Ne'ilah*. He was overcome with grief that he had slept through all of the holy day, and wept profusely as he recited the *Ne'ilah* prayers.

After the close of the fast, R' Pinchas asked R' David, "Who is the young man who prayed so fervently during *Ne'ilah*? The prosecuting angels were bringing harsh accusations against Israel, but this young man's tears washed them all away."

The Talmud says that the pious people of yore would meditate a full hour before praying (*Berachos* 30b). Developing a sincere attitude in prayer and bonding with Hashem produces *simchah shel mitzvah*.

11
TZEDAKAH AND GEMILAS CHASSADIM

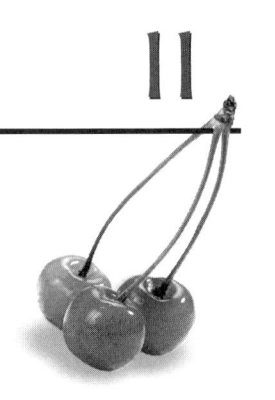

The character-refining potential of *tzedakah* hardly needs elaboration. Man's animal nature is selfish and egocentric. *Tzedakah* is the very antithesis of selfishness and egocentricity, and contributes substantially to development of the uniquely human traits that elevate man above other living creatures. Inasmuch as *tzedakah* contributes to self-fulfillment, it is reason for simchah.

R' Meir of Premishlan was lavish with giving *tzedakah*. He explained that one man came before the Heavenly Tribunal requesting admission to *Gan Eden* (Paradise). "By what merit?" he was asked. "I learned much Torah," he said. The tribunal remarked, "You studied Torah for ulterior motives. You wished to be respected as a scholar. You used Torah study for ego purposes. That does not warrant *Gan Eden*."

Another person was asked what was his claim to *Gan Eden*. "I *davened* every day," he said. The tribunal remarked, "When you *davened*, you did not have proper *kavannah* (concentration). Your thoughts wandered off to all your business affairs. That does not warrant *Gan Eden*."

A third person said that his claim to *Gan Eden* was that he gave *tzedakah*. The gates promptly swung open for him. The tribunal did not investigate his reasons for giving *tzedakah* because these were irrelevant. The fact was that he helped put food on the tables of the needy and clothes on their children. That is an undeniable merit.

"And so," R' Meir said, "I want to have merits that need not be investigated. That is why I give *tzedakah*."

Doing a mitzvah whose reward is guaranteed is reason for simchah.

What a privilege it is to give *tzedakah*! A person who had recovered from alcoholism and who willingly helped many others recover was asked, "Doesn't it annoy you when someone calls for help at 2 a.m. ?" He responded, "No way! I'm grateful that I'm not the one who is doing the calling." The mitzvah of *tzedakah* is so great that the Midrash says that the donor is actually a greater beneficiary than the recipient (*Vayikra Rabbah* 34:10). When someone knocks on the door requesting *tzedakah*, the attitude, "Oh, another *schnorrer*," compromises this great mitzvah. Even if not verbalized, the recipient feels the disparagement. At the very least, one should be thankful that one can be a donor and not a recipient of *tzedakah*.

While all *tzedakah* is self-fulfilling and meritorious, the manner in which it is given is also important. The Talmud requires sensitivity to the feelings of the person who must have recourse to *tzedakah*. Although giving *tzedakah* in any way is commendable, giving it in a way that can elevate the spirits of the recipient is especially meritorious. "One who gives *tzedakah* receives six blessings, and one who comforts the recipient of *tzedakah* receives eleven blessings" (*Bava Basra* 9b). Receiving blessings is certainly reason for simchah, as is the knowledge that you have been helpful to others.

Giving *tzedakah* in a way that the donor and recipient are unknown to each other spares the latter's embarrassment. Furthermore, the donor does not develop feelings of magnanimity. *Matan beseisser*, secret giving, is, therefore, considered the highest form of *tzedakah*.

There are numerous accounts of *matan beseisser*. In one community, meat and bread were distributed to the poor every Friday. There was a wealthy miser in town who never gave *tzedakah*, but when he died, the weekly distribution of the meat and bread stopped. The butcher and baker then revealed that the "tightwad" had secretly provided the money for the meat and bread, but had sworn those who distributed them to secrecy as to its source. At the time he died, this was not known, and because of his reputation as a miser, he was not buried in a respectable place in the cemetery. When his secret was discovered, Rabbi Yom Tov Heller (*Tosafos Yom Tov*) left a will that he be buried next to the "miser," who was a hidden *tzaddik*.

A beautiful example of *matan beseisser* is a practice of the Jewish community in Berlin. There were mourners, who, because they were unable to work in the week of *shivah*, needed financial help. On the first day of *shivah*, two *pushkes* (*tzedakah* boxes) were delivered to the mourners, one containing money and the other empty. The mourners were to take the money from the first *pushke* for their use. If any money remained, they put it in the second *pushke*, which also served as the receptacle for *tzedakah* contributed by people who made condolence visits. After the *shivah*, the *pushkes* were returned. In this way, no one had any idea whether or how much of the money the mourners had used.

The *tzaddik* of Sanz did not discriminate with *tzedakah*. One time, people chastised him for giving *tzedakah* to a scoundrel. "He certainly does not deserve it," they said.

The *tzaddik* responded, "We know that Hashem acts toward us the way we behave toward others. If I give money to someone who does not deserve it, I can hope that Hashem will give to me even though I don't deserve it. But if I give only to people who deserve it, what right do I have to ask Hashem for anything for myself?"

If giving *tzedakah* to all needy people earns one special favor from Hashem, is that not reason for simchah?

Tzedakah is a mitzvah that every person can perform. No special preparations are needed. One does not even recite a *berachah* for this great mitzvah. It is within everyone's reach.

A group of chassidim who wished to spend Shabbos with the Seer of Lublin hired Chaikel, a wagon-driver to drive them. Chaikel was a boor, the simplest of the simple, and he did not understand a single word of the chassidim's conversation. Shortly before arriving in Lublin, he saw the chassidim writing on small scraps of paper. They explained to Chaikel that they were writing a *kvittel*, a petition to the rebbe, asking for his blessing. Chaikel asked the chassidim to write a *kvittel* for him, too, and as is traditional, gave them his full name and his mother's name.

It was a while before the chassidim gained an audience with the Seer. After submitting their *kvitlach,* they gave the Seer the *kvittel* bearing Chaikel's name. As the Seer read the *kvittel,* he exclaimed, "Who is this *tzaddik* whose mitzvah has illuminated the heavens?" The chassidim did not know what to make of it. Chaikel, a *tzaddik*? Could it be that Chaikel was one of the hidden *tzaddikim*?

The chassidim spread out through Lublin, to see if they could find this "hidden *tzaddik.*" Passing one inn, they heard lively music, and on entering the inn, they found a wedding party, and Chaikel was dancing on the table, rousing all the guests to merriment.

"Tell us the truth about yourself," the chassidim said to Chaikel. "You can no longer conceal your identity. We know that you are one of the hidden *tzaddikim*!" Chaikel laughed. "Me, a *tzaddik*? You must be out of your mind!"

"What are you doing at this wedding party?" the chassidim asked.

"After dropping you off," Chaikel said, "I came to this inn for a bit of food and some beer. I found a small wedding party, but everyone was sad. The *kallah* is a poor orphan, and the townsfolk

11: Tzedakah and Gemilas Chassadim / 79

had promised her a dowry. When they failed to show up with the money, the *chasan* said that he was not going to go ahead with the wedding. The *kallah's* tears broke my heart, so I took the bag of money I had with me and said, "Here is your dowry!" They went ahead with the wedding, and I stayed on to make merry!"

You can have a mitzvah that glows with a brightness that illuminates the heavens: *tzedakah.*

It is related that the Heavenly Tribunal gave a huge reward in *Gan Eden* to a man who gave *tzedakah,* explaining that his *tzedakah* had enabled a person to survive. As a result, that person was able to support his family, and all the merits accrued by the family for the mitzvos they did could be added to his account. On the other hand, a person who stole something because he was hungry was given a mild punishment. Satan objected that this was not just, and that the long-range harm done by the thief should be charged against him.

The Heavenly Tribunal explained, "If the man who gave the *tzedakah* had been asked, he would certainly have said that he wanted his *tzedakah* to have long-range beneficial effects. However, had you asked the thief, he would have said that he really did not want to cause anyone suffering, and that he stole only because he was hungry. If he could have gotten food any other way, he would not have stolen. There was no reason to punish him for any long-range consequences of his sin.

Gemilas chassadim is akin to *tzedakah,* in that both are an extension of help to others. The Talmud rates *gemilas chassadim* even more meritorious than *tzedakah,* because whereas *tzedakah* is with one's belongings, *gemilas chassadim* is with one's person (*Succah* 49b). Indeed, Maharsha states that *gemilas chassadim* is the greatest of *all* mitzvos (ibid.). *Midrash Hagadol* says that a person who performs *gemilas chassadim* is as if he fulfilled the Ten Commandments (23:20).

Essentially, Judaism is founded on *gemilas chassadim.* This was the outstanding character trait of the patriarch Abraham, father of the Jewish nation. The patriarch, three days after circumcising himself at the age of 99, and undoubtedly in severe pain, sat at the door of his tent in the torrid heat of the midday sun, looking for wayfarers for whom he might provide food and drink. *Gemilas chassadim* is considered so basic to the essence of Judaism that lack of *gemilas chassadim* raises doubts as to a person's Jewish identity (*Yevamos* 78b).

We usually think of *gemilas chassadim* in terms of visiting the sick (*bikur cholim*), extending hospitality to strangers and wayfarers (*hachnassas orchim*), paying our respects at a funeral (*levayas hameis*), enabling a bride to be married (*hachnassas kallah*), and making condolence calls (*nichum aveilim*). These are, of course, prime examples of *gemilas chassadim*, but there are countless opportunities every day for performing this mitzvah. Helping an elderly person climb the stairs, giving a person a lift, or getting an item for someone that is beyond his reach is *gemilas chassadim*. Volunteering in a nursing home or hospital, and trying to comfort the sick or feeble in any way, is *gemilas chassadim*. Anything that comforts a person or makes things easier for him, even giving someone in shul a *siddur* or *Chumash,* is *gemilas chassadim.*

Any time a person can make someone feel good, that is a mitzvah of *gemilas chassadim.*

When R' Yisrael of Salant was Rosh Yeshivah in Vilna, there was a young man who spent part of the day in business. At one point he suffered a financial loss and was depressed. One time he confronted the scholars in the yeshivah with a very difficult problem in the Talmud, which none of the scholars could resolve.

When R' Yisrael entered, they posed the problem to him. R' Yisrael deliberated over the problem, then said, "I cannot find a solution to this problem. The young man has posed a very difficult question." After the young man left, R' Yisrael told the other scholars the solution to the problem. "You see," he said, "this young man has been depressed because of his loss of money. I wanted to lift his spirits a bit. Now he feels that he has discovered a problem which even the Rosh Yeshivah cannot resolve. That will give him a sense of pride, and he will feel a bit better."

The Chafetz Chaim used to say that *gemilas chassadim* embraces all interpersonal relations. "Practicing *gemilas chassadim* can protect a person from ever offending someone else and can bring a person to many good deeds."

As important as learning from *sefarim* is, we must have recourse to actual life-experiences of our *gedolim*, because their understanding of things may be significantly different than ours. Here is an example of this.

Suppose you have done someone a favor, and he thanks you for it. Some people respond, "Oh, don't mention it. It was really nothing." R' Yeruchem Levovitz says that you must be honest with yourself. Are you saying this because in all sincerity you wanted to do a favor for that person, or is it possible that you are dismissing his gratitude because you want him to feel beholden to you?

R' Yeruchem says that it is a *gemilas chesed* to let that person do a favor for *you*. This enables him to be alleviated of the feeling of being indebted to you.

One of the benefits of *gemilas chassadim* is that it contributes greatly to character refinement. Self-centeredness is a major character defect that has many serious behavioral consequences. *Gemilas chassadim* is the antithesis of self-centeredness, and the more that one does for others, the less preoccupied one is with self-gratification.

The reward for *tzedakah* and *gemilas chassadim* is immeasurable. There are many mundane pleasures, but even the most tasty delicacies do not provide for more than a transient delight. But if you have given *tzedakah* or done *gemilas chesed*, you can relish the pleasure of having helped someone in need, even after the passing of many years. This awareness and pleasure is cause for simchah.

12

Bircas HaMazon (Blessing After Meals)

On Yom Kippur eve, the shuls are crowded for *Kol Nidrei*. For some people, this may be the only time in the year that they come to shul. People are garbed in white *kittels* and are wearing *taleisim*. The atmosphere is solemn.

True, it is the onset of Yom Kippur. The solemnity of the strains of the *Kol Nidrei* prayer are said to go back to the days of the Inquisition, when Jews were coerced, under penalty of death, to take a vow asserting their loyalty to Christianity. Jews gathered in utmost secrecy and recited *Kol Nidrei*, annulling this vow.

That is what *Kol Nidrei* is: an abrogation of vows that one may have made during the year. It is hardly a prayer of comparatively great import. Many people abrogate their vows before Rosh

Hashanah. It is not even a prayer for forgiveness. Yet, which Jew would miss *Kol Nidrei?* Undoubtedly, many people believe that it is the most important prayer in the Jewish liturgy.

Surprise! It is not! *Kol Nidrei* originated centuries after formulation of the *Amidah* by the Sages of the Great Assembly. But even the prayer of the *Amidah* is of rabbinic origin. There is only one prayer that is of unquestionable Scriptural origin: *Bircas HaMazon*: "You shall eat and be satisfied, and you shall thank G-d" (*Deuteronomy* 8:10). *Bircas HaMazon* (Blessing After Meals) is, therefore, the most important prayer in the Jewish liturgy. One might think that *Bircas HaMazon* would be recited with at least the *kavannah* given to *Kol Nidrei*. Alas! Just the opposite is true. *Bircas HaMazon* is often hurriedly rattled off after one has finished the last course of the meal and one is rushing off to some activity. *Bircas HaMazon* has not been accorded its due.

Bircas HaMazon is an expression of gratitude, thanking Hashem not only for the food we have eaten, but also for the holy land of Eretz Yisrael bequeathed to the patriarchs, for our deliverance from the enslavement in Egypt, for the mitzvah of *milah* (circumcision), and for the mitzvos of the Torah. In addition, *Bircas HaMazon* is also an expression of faith and trust in Hashem, that He will always provide for us.

Inasmuch as the mitzvos are intended to refine a person's character, *Bircas HaMazon* may very well lead the way toward this goal. *Hakaras hatov*, gratitude, acknowledgment, and appreciation of a kindness is foremost in the attainment of proper *middos*. One of Moses' sharpest reprimand, to the Israelites was that they were ingrates (*Avodah Zarah* 5a).

The extraordinary importance of *hakaras hatov* can be gathered from the Midrash, that when Hashem commanded Moses to go to Egypt to deliver the Israelites, Moses said, "I must take leave from my father-in-law, Jethro, who took me in when I was a fugitive from Pharaoh. I owe him this respect." Why did Moses delay following the Divine commandment? Because Moses knew that Hashem expected him to practice *hakaras hatov*.

Many people seem to have difficulty in expressing gratitude. *Tosafos* (ibid.) says that the Israelites' reluctance to express gratitude to Hashem was because they did not wish to be behold-en to Him. This explains why a person may not even *acknowledge* a kindness. Whatever the reason, it is important that a person overcome this resistance. Saying *Bircas HaMazon* several times a day with proper *kavannah* helps one develop the salutary trait of *hakaras hatov*.

The commandment of *Bircas HaMazon* as noted is explicitly spelled out in the Torah. The text was composed by Moses, Joshua, David, and Solomon. The first paragraph was composed by Moses when the Israelites received the miraculous manna.

We commemorate the manna not only in *Bircas HaMazon*, but also on Friday night, when we recite the blessing of *hamotzi* over two challahs, representing the double portion of manna that the Israelites received on Friday. Covering the challahs represents the dew that covered the manna (*Exodus* 16:13).

R' Mendel of Rimanov says that the manna preceded the giving of the Torah at Sinai because it was essential that the Israelites believe that Hashem will provide everyone with sustenance according to his need, and that one gains nothing by hoarding. Without this conviction, the innate human acquisitive drive would have made it difficult to accept the many laws that restrict unfair enrichment, whether by theft, deceit, or usury. This conviction is vital in the modern commercial world, if one is to conduct oneself honestly.

A merchant complained to R' Mendel that someone was opening a competing store in close proximity to his shop, and he was afraid that this would compromise his income. R' Mendel told him that when a horse drinks from a stream, he taps with his hoof. This is because when he sees his reflection in the water, he thinks that another horse is there, and he wants to drive it away lest it drink up the water. "Don't behave like a horse. No one can take from you what Hashem has destined for you."

Reflecting on the lesson of the manna in *Bircas HaMazon* should enable a person not only to transact honestly but also not to feel deprived or envious of what others may have. A person who feels he is lacking is not happy. The conviction that "Hashem is giving me my true needs" is reason for simchah.

Although the Scriptural obligation of *Bircas HaMazon* is only when one has eaten to satiety, rabbinic ordinance expands this obligation to having eaten even a small quantity of bread, no greater than the size of an egg. The Talmud says that we merit abundant blessings because we thank Hashem even when we have not eaten to satiety (*Berachos* 20b).

Joshua composed the second paragraph of *Bircas HaMazon* when the Israelites entered the Promised Land. Moses had cautioned them, "Lest you eat and be satiated...and you may say 'My might and the strength of my hand has brought me this wealth.' Then you shall remember that it is Hashem Who gives you the ability to acquire wealth" (*Deuteronomy* 8:17-18). This paragraph should remind us that our success in amassing belongings is not due to our own effort, but to the blessing of Hashem in what we do.

The third *berachah* begins with a prayer for restoration of Jerusalem and the Temple, and continues with a prayer for Divine sustenance. When Solomon dedicated the Temple, he said, "When Your people return to You with all their hearts and all their souls in the lands of their enemies to which they have been taken captive, and they will pray to You through the land that You gave to their ancestors, the city that You have chosen, and the House that I built to Your Name, then You, in Heaven, will hear their prayer" (*I Kings* 8:48-49). Inasmuch as our prayers are directed toward Jerusalem, we follow the prayer for restoration of Jerusalem with a prayer that Hashem continue to provide for our needs.

David composed the paragraph of gratitude for Jerusalem, and Solomon added the verse for the Temple. Following the destruction of the Temple, the wording of this paragraph was changed by Ezra the Scribe to be a prayer for Hashem's mercy to restore the glory of Jerusalem and the Temple.

The final paragraph of *Bircas HaMazon* was added much later. After the fall of Beitar to the Romans, the Jews were unable to retrieve the bodies of those who had fallen in the battle. When they were finally able to do so, they found the bodies to be fully preserved and they were able to give them a proper burial. The sages then composed a brief prayer, thanking Hashem for this kindness, and although it has no relationship to a meal, they appended it to *Bircas HaMazon* because this was a prayer that is recited daily. The teaching in this is that even when one experiences adversity, one should know that one has not lost the favor of Hashem. This is an uplifting thought when one experiences distress, and even though it may not produce the simchah of joy, it can produce the second aspect of simchah, the simchah of acceptance with serenity.

How different our lives would be if we implemented all the teachings of *Bircas HaMazon!* So much is unfortunately lost when one says *Bircas HaMazon* hurriedly, giving little thought even to the meaning of the words, let alone to the teachings they convey.

When Hashem pronounced the punishment for the transgression of the fruit of the Tree of Knowledge, He said to the serpent, "You shall eat dust all the days of your life" (*Genesis* 3:14). The commentaries ask, "What kind of a punishment is it that a serpent has an inexhaustible food supply?" They answer, The fact that man must pray to Hashem for his sustenance brings him into a relationship with Hashem. To the serpent Hashem said, "You will never have to turn to Me for your food. You are so despicable that I don't even wish to hear your prayers." The Ari z"l says that *Bircas HaMazon* should be said with the simchah that one is fulfilling a mitzvah. Our prayers for food indicate that Hashem wants a relationship with us, and that is reason for joy.

When three people eat together, *Bircas HaMazon* is introduced with an invitation, "Let us thank Hashem," to which the response is, "May the Name of Hashem be blessed from now unto eternity." The leader then says, "Let us thank Him from Whose bounty we have eaten," and the others respond, "Blessed is He from Whose bounty we have eaten and with His goodness we live." The Midrash attributes this to the patriarch Abraham, who provided food to hungry wayfarers. When they thanked him for the food, Abraham said, "Do not thank me. Thank the One Who is the Provider of food." In this way Abraham promulgated the recognition of Hashem. This is a teaching for us to follow in the footsteps of the patriarch and to behave in a manner that will bring greater glory to the Name of Hashem.

Saying *Bircas HaMazon* with proper *kavannah* and adopting its teachings can certainly result in simchah.

13
Mezuzah

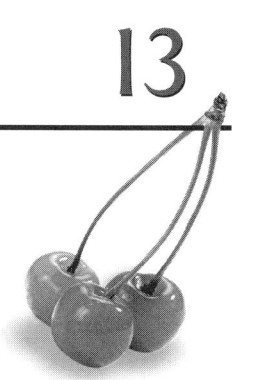

The *mezuzah* affixed to the doorpost contains two paragraphs of the *Shema* that declare the unity of Hashem, that we are to love Hashem with all our heart and soul, and that our observance of the mitzvos will merit Hashem's blessing.

The Talmud states that *ve'ahavta es Hashem* means not only that we are to love Hashem, but also that we are to make Hashem beloved by others, by behaving honestly and courteously (*Yoma* 86a). As we leave our homes to interact with people and transact with them, we should remember that we must do so in a manner that will cause people to respect Hashem and the Torah. When we return home, even after a stressful day at work, we must act within the family in a way that will increase love of Hashem by members of the family.

A Torah-observant Jew must be committed to *avodas Hashem*. While this is usually translated to mean "serving Hashem," it would be well to remember that *avodah* means "work." A person may have to exert himself in order to serve Hashem. The *Shema* constitutes *ol malchus shamayim*, acceptance of the *yoke* of heaven. If a person comes home from work after an aggravating day at the office, and the spouse or child says or does something that is irritating, a natural response may be an angry outburst. Suppressing the natural response and exerting control so that one remains calm may require much effort. When a Torah-observant person explodes with rage, this indicates that Torah observance has not influenced one's *middos*, and this detracts from respect for Torah and love of Hashem. *Avodas Hashem* requires that a person exert the necessary effort to suppress one's rage. Such behavior, both within and outside the home, can prevent the aggravation that interferes with simchah.

The *mezuzah* is, of course, a protection for the home. Onkelos bar Klonimus, a nephew of the emperor, converted to Judaism. When the emperor sent a contingency of soldiers to dissuade him, Onkelos said, "A secular king sits in his inner chambers, and his soldiers stand guard at the doors. With Jews, it is just the reverse. The people live inside the home, and Hashem, their King, stands guard at the doors" (*Avodah Zarah* 11a).

The *mezuzah* should also be seen as a sign of welcome, so that passersby should know that this is a Jewish home.

We often see people entering a room, touching the *mezuzah*, and kissing the fingertips that had come in contact with the *mezuzah*. This is indeed a beautiful gesture, but it would take on so much more meaning if one spent just a few moments with one's hand on the *mezuzah*, reflecting on its contents and their implication for how one should behave. Affixing a *mezuzah* to the doorpost is indeed a great mitzvah. Incorporating the words of the *mezuzah* in our hearts can lead to simchah.

The *mezuzah* conveys yet another important message. Some halachic authorities require that the *mezuzah* be affixed in a vertical position, while others say it should be affixed horizontally.

The practice of affixing the *mezuzah* diagonally is a compromise between the two. Looking at the *mezuzah* should remind us that it is often wise to compromise, rather than to be obstinate in holding to one's position. This flexibility can eliminate the squabbles that may interfere with simchah.

14

The Shofar and Rosh Hashanah

The mitzvah of shofar is generally seen as a clarion call, arousing a person from the routine and tedium of daily life, to do a *cheshbon hanefesh,* a personal reckoning. It is obvious that a fearless inventory of oneself can enable a person to discover defects of character which need to be addressed and corrected. If we think of the shofar this way, this mitzvah is certainly conducive to character refinement and achievement of simchah.

It is interesting to note the marked difference between our celebration of Rosh Hashanah and the secular New Year. On December 31, many people get together to celebrate with hilarity and much imbibing of alcoholic beverages. Many people are intoxicated when the clock strikes 12 and the new calendar year begins, and declare loudly, "Happy New Year." But are they really as happy as they appear to be?

Alcohol does give a person a feeling of relaxation, but it does so because it is essentially an anesthetic. Alcohol dulls a person's senses, so that he is less aware of the many things that are distressing to him. It follows that if a person is experiencing a feeling of happiness, the last thing one would want to do is to dull that sensation. Why, then, must people be intoxicated to exclaim "Happy New Year"? Aren't they happy about the advent of the new year?

Life is generally a series of days, with any one day being quite similar to any other day. People fall into a rut, and rarely take the time to think about what they have accomplished and where they stand in pursuit of their goal in life, if indeed they *have* a goal in life.

But there are times when our routine is interrupted, and we may be shocked into contemplating what our lives are all about. One such time is New Year's Eve. "What do you mean it is 2007? I've just gotten over the habit of dating my checks 2006, and it's 2007 already! Whatever happened to 2006? A whole year has flown by! I'm one year older (and by that token, a year of my life is irretrievably gone). What do I have to show for being one year older? Am I much wiser? Hardly. Am I better off financially? No way! I'm deeper in debt than ever. Do I have any reason to believe that next year is going to be appreciably more profitable? No."

This awareness is depressing, and can put one into a very dismal mood. How can one be happy when he realizes that the past year was essentially wasted and the prospects for the coming year are not any better? There is only one way one can celebrate the New Year, and that is by blotting out the depressing awareness, and this is most effectively accomplished by alcohol. So, people get drunk on New Year's Eve, and in the state of obtunded awareness, declare, "Happy New Year!" Why, if they were not intoxicated, they would be crying.

Rosh Hashanah is radically different. For the past 30 days of Elul, we have been making a *cheshbon hanefesh,* carefully reviewing the events of the past year, seeing where we had erred and resolving to improve on our character defects. We know that we are standing before Hashem, the Judge from Whom we cannot conceal anything, Who knows our innermost thoughts and Whom we cannot deceive. We know that the sincerity of our *teshuvah* will determine our judgment. Recognition of the mistakes of the past year turns them into positive learning experiences, which makes the past year a profitable one. We have reason to look forward to a better year, and that Hashem will inscribe us for a year of life, health and prosperity. We have no reason to escape from our feelings, and with maximum awareness we can wish others and accept their wish of "*Shana Tovah,*" in a completely sober and happy state.

Rosh Hashanah is indeed a solemn day, but it is also a festival. The prophet says of Rosh Hashanah, "Eat delicacies and drink sweets, and send portions to those who do not have, because this day is holy to our Master. Do not be sad, because the joy of Hashem is your strength" (*Nehemiah* 8:10). While it is not a day of levity, it is a day of simchah.

There is an aspect of shofar that should add to our simchah. The Maggid of Dubnow relates a parable of a king who went foxhunting, but separated from his retinue and was lost in the forest. Soon it became dark, and a heavy rain fell. In the distance he saw a dim light, and heading toward that light he found a hut of a woodsman, who welcomed him, gave him dry clothes, food, and a hot drink, and assured him that in the morning he would show him the way out of the forest.

Arriving at the palace, the king was very grateful, and rewarded the woodsman with an honorable position in the palace. Several years later, the woodsman foolishly allowed himself to be drawn into a conspiracy, and when the conspirators were arrested, they were sentenced to death, the woodsman among them.

Before their execution, the conspirators were allowed a last request. The woodsman asked to be allowed to put on his woodsman's clothes and appear before the king. When he did so, the king was reminded how the woodsman had saved him and been kind to him, and he gave him a pardon.

"So it is with us," the Maggid of Dubnow said. "Hashem went around to all the peoples of the world, offering them the Torah, but they all rejected Him. Only we, the Jewish people, gladly accepted His sovereignty at Sinai by declaring *naaseh venishma* (we shall do and we shall listen), expressing our unequivocal subjugation to Hashem's will, and enthroning him as our king.

"The Torah was given at Sinai amid the sounding of the shofar (*Exodus* 19:19). When we sound the shofar on Rosh Hashonah, we 'remind' Hashem that we were the only people who accepted Him as our King. That is adequate reason for giving us a favorable judgment."

Being secure in receiving a favorable judgment, the shofar should bring us simchah.

There is a *minhag* (custom) to go to a body of water (lake, ocean, river) on Rosh Hashanah and recite prayers for forgiveness. This ritual is referred to as *tashlich*, which means to "cast away." A popular assumption is that one casts away one's sins into the water.

This is erroneous. The only way to divest oneself of sins is to do a thorough and sincere *teshuvah*. One cannot rid oneself of sins by throwing them into the water.

In the prayer of *tashlich*, we recite the verse, that Hashem "will again be merciful to us. He will suppress our iniquities, and You will cast (*tashlich*) **into the sea** all their sins" (*Micah* 7:19). Some add the verse "And all the sins of Your nation, the House of Israel, cast away (*tashlich*) to a place where they will neither be remembered, considered, nor brought to mind — ever."

The ritual of *tashlich* is an affirmation that when one has done a sincere *teshuvah*, Hashem's forgiveness will remove all traces of one's sins, as the prophet says, "I will erase your willful sins like a cloud and your errors like a fog" (*Isaiah* 44:22). It is important that one should not carry a burden of guilt, but should have faith that, with proper *teshuvah*, Hashem's forgiveness is absolute. It is not *we* that throw our sins into the water, but rather Hashem, Who erases our sins and casts them into the depth of the sea, never to be retrieved.

All our sins not only are forgiven, but totally erased, never to be remembered. Is that not reason to rejoice? We can see why the prophet said, "Do not be sad, because the joy of Hashem is your strength."

The Talmud says that on Rosh Hashanah, a judgment is issued on every individual for the coming year. On the other hand, the Talmud says that a person is judged every day. The Baal Shem Tov's students asked him how these apparently conflicting statements can be reconciled.

The Baal Shem Tov looked out the window and saw Chaikel, the water carrier. "Come here, Chaikel," the Baal Shem Tov said.

"How are things with you, Chaikel?" the Baal Shem Tov asked.

Chaikel sighed. "Not good, Rebbe," he said. "At my age, I still have to shlep buckets of water up the hill to make a living." The Baal Shem Tov wished him well and dismissed him.

Several days later, the Baal Shem Tov was sitting with his students and saw Chaikel carrying buckets of water. "How are things with you, Chaikel?" the Baal Shem Tov asked.

Chaikel smiled. "Thank G-d, Rebbe. At my age, I can still shlep buckets of water up the hill."

The Baal Shem Tov said to his students, "There is your answer. On Rosh Hashanah it was decreed that Chaikel would earn his livelihood by carrying water. But how Chaikel accepts that judgment may vary from day to day. A person passes judgment on himself every day."

Many circumstances are not within our control, but it is our choice whether or not to have simchah.

15

YOM KIPPUR — A FRESH START

The Talmud says that Hashem created the concept of *teshuvah* prior to creating the world (*Nedarim* 39b). His intent was that the world should be populated by human beings rather than by heavenly angels, and human beings are fallible. If there was no way in which a human being could divest himself of the guilt for having done wrong, man would be so burdened by guilt that a productive life would be impossible.

Suppose that once in a century there would be a day of amnesty on which all one's sins would be forgiven. If the "amnesty day" occurred, say in the year 2000, a person born within a few years of the "amnesty day" would feel deprived, because he was unlikely to live until the next day of forgiveness in 2100. Even a person who was born in 2060 would realize that only the sins up to age 40 would be forgiven by the next amnesty day. Only people born between 2020 and 2030 could realistically look forward to a day on which the sins in the greater part of their lives would be forgiven.

How fortunate we are that we have an "amnesty day" every year! We can have a fresh start on life every year.

A person who unfortunately committed many sins may despair of changing his lifestyle. He may say, "What's the use? I've done so many wrong things that I cannot redeem myself regardless of how hard I try." This obstacle is eliminated by Yom Kippur. With a desire to correct things, all the sins of the past are forgiven.

Of course, Yom Kippur eradicates only those sins that involved our relationship with our Maker and that were not offensive to another person. For the latter sins, one must make amends, apologizing and asking for forgiveness, and where necessary, making restitution. Do you know how good a feeling it is when one has apologized? That can be a feeling of real simchah.

Halachah requires that a person who is asked to forgive should do so. After all, are we not asking Hashem to forgive us? The Baal Shem Tov cited the verse in *Psalms* (121:5), "Hashem is your shadow," and commented that just as one's shadow mimics one's every move, so Hashem relates to a person corresponding to how the person relates to others. If one forgives others, then Hashem forgives him. Granting forgiveness means receiving forgiveness, and that, too, is a reason for joy.

"But," one may say, "it is so difficult to forgive someone who has hurt or offended me." Granted, but just what can you do with the grudge you carry against that person? The Torah explicitly forbids not only taking revenge, but even saying to the person if he is in need of help, "I will do it for you, even though you don't deserve it." A grudge is nothing but excess baggage that weighs down on you. The person who offended you could not care less how you feel about him. He has stopped thinking about you long ago. You are the one suffering the consequences of hanging on to a resentment. It is in your own interest to forgive.

You can learn how to forgive by practicing forgiveness. Verbalizing the words is not enough. Try to do something nice for the person whom you resent. You will then feel forgiveness, get a load off your heart, and you will feel 10 feet tall. Forgiving can provide a feeling of simchah.

As was noted earlier, *somei'ach* is related to *tzomei'ach*; growth and happiness are intertwined. *Teshuvah* and forgiving are opportunities for spiritual growth. Rambam explains that the dynamics of *teshuvah* are that the person undergoes a character change so that he is no longer the same person who committed the sin. This "new" person is not accountable for what the other, "old" person did.

Proper *teshuvah* is, therefore, more than remorse. It is even more than resolving never to repeat the act. A sin does not occur in a vacuum. A person commits a sin only when one is at a particular level of spirituality that makes commission of that sin possible. Proper *teshuvah* means elevating oneself to a level of spirituality where that sin is no longer a possibility. Hence, *teshuvah* requires a character change, and Rambam rightly states that with this kind of *teshuvah* one is transformed into a different person.

There is a difference between the feelings of "guilt" and "shame." Guilt is a feeling one has for having done wrong. By regretting what one has done and elevating oneself to a level of spirituality that makes it impossible to repeat the wrong deed, one can divest oneself of the guilt and have a feeling of simchah on being this new individual.

"Shame" is not merely a feeling of having done wrong. Shame is a feeling that one is inherently *bad*. This may result from a child being told "You're bad" or the equivalent, and the child may develop the feeling that he *is* somehow bad. To put it aptly, guilt is the feeling, "I *made* a mistake," whereas shame is the feeling, "I *am* a mistake." *Teshuvah* can effectively relieve guilt, because it relates to a deed. Inasmuch as shame is the feeling that one is inherently defective, *teshuvah* does not remove this feeling. Shame can be relieved only by a person concluding that he is not inherently bad. This may be accomplished by self-help with some guidance, or may require therapy.

15: Yom Kippur—a Fresh Start / 99

Parenthetically, it is important that while children require discipline, parents should be most careful not to use expressions that could give the child the feeling that he is bad. When my father disapproved of something I had done, he would say, "*Es past nisht*" (that is not becoming of you). He was not telling me that I was bad, but to the contrary, I was too good to be doing something that was beneath my dignity.

Prior to *Kol Nidrei*, most people have a very solemn demeanor. Sometimes they may weep profusely. R' Moshe of Kobrin was critical of this. "The solemnity of Yom Kippur should not result in sadness," he said. "The Talmud says that on Yom Kippur, Hashem silences Satan and does not allow him to enter accusations against Israel. Therefore, Satan takes advantage of the moments before Yom Kippur, before he is deprived of his powers, to cast people into depression. True, a person should be broken hearted because of one's sins, but should be happy in the knowledge that these will be forgiven."

How can we be certain that we will be forgiven? R' Levi Yitzchak of Berditchev said that in the Yom Kippur prayers we recite a *berachah*, "Blessed are You, Hashem, Who forgives and pardons our sins, and removes our transgressions every year." R' Levi Yitzchak told of a child who brought some cookies to *cheder*, and when another child asked him for a cookie, he refused to share with him. The other child then recited the *berachah* for a cookie. The child with the cookies could not allow a *berachah* to be said in vain, so he had no choice but to give the other child a cookie.

"That is what we do," R' Levi Yitzchak said. "We recite the *berachah* that Hashem forgives our sins each year. If He were not to forgive us, the *berachah* would be in vain. To prevent that, Hashem forgives our sins."

The relief of guilt resulting from *teshuvah*, and the knowledge that one has a fresh start in life, is reason for simchah.

16

Succos and the Four Species

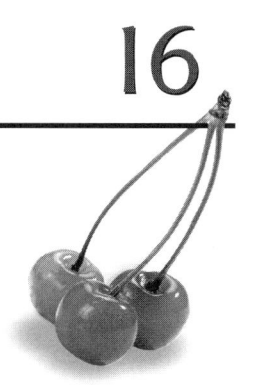

Succah is a mitzvah that is to be celebrated with much simchah. One *tzaddik* said, "The mitzvah of *succah* is truly all encompassing. All other mitzvos we do with just part of the body, but we enter into this mitzvah even with our boots."

There is a difference of opinion among the sages of the Mishnah as to the significance of the *succah*. Although we generally do not seek reasons for the mitzvos, *succah* is an exception. The Torah explicitly states that the reason for the *succah* is "so that your generations should know that I settled the children of Israel in *succos* when I delivered them from the land of Egypt" (*Leviticus* 23:42).

Yes, but to what is the verse referring by *"succos"*? R' Akiva takes the word *succah* literally: during the sojourn in the desert, the Israelites lived in thatched huts, and this is what we commemorate. R' Eliezer says that the *succos* in the verse refers to the miraculous Clouds of Glory that surrounded the Israelites and protected them throughout their 40 years in the desert. The prevailing opinion is that of R' Eliezer.

R' Eliezer's version explains why we celebrate the festival. Miraculous, protective Clouds of Glory certainly deserve being commemorated. But according to R' Akiva, what is so special about the fact that the Israelites lived in temporary huts that is worthy of commemorating?

We may understand this with an episode in R' Akiva's life. In his young years, R' Akiva was illiterate and completely ignorant of Torah. Rachel, the beautiful daughter of the wealthy Kalba Savua, recognized the potential in this great man and married him, whereupon her irate father disowned and banished her. The couple were impoverished, and lived in a barn. The prophet Elijah appeared to them disguised as a beggar, asking if they could spare some straw for his wife, who was in labor and had nothing on which to rest. R' Akiva said to Rachel, "See! There are people who are less fortunate than us."

R' Akiva recognized that one should be grateful for having a bed of straw. He believed that having a temporary hut is cause for gratitude.

Many commentaries interpret the seven days that we dwell in the temporary *succah* as representing the seven decades of the average life span of man on earth, which is a temporary dwelling, in which we prepare ourselves for an existence in a permanent, eternal home. If the *succah* represents our mortality, one would hardly consider Succos to be a joyous festival. Rather, it would appear to be rather morose.

Not so. A bit of reflection should reveal that if all there is to human life is mundane, then our existence is a rather sordid affair. Much of mankind experiences at least some suffering, and many people suffer a great deal. If there are a fortunate few who escape misery, they face the unpleasantness so common in the later years of life, and, ultimately, the prospect of death.

But if we understand that our true, eternal existence is in the World to Come, and our sojourn on earth is but preparatory for our eternal lives, then life takes on a profound meaning. We have the opportunity to accumulate merits that will enhance our eternal bliss.

The Torah refers to Succos as "the festival of harvest" (*Exodus* 34:32, *Deuteronomy* 16:13). True, there is joy in bringing in an abundant harvest, but we must remember that earthly possessions do not give enduring simchah. It is precisely at this time that we must be reminded that there is more to life than accumulation of earthly goods. Certainly, we should enjoy these and be thankful to Hashem for His bounty, but the real reason for joy is that we have the opportunity for an eternal life of spiritual bliss.

On Succos, we welcome the *ushpizin* (guests) into our *succah*: Abraham, Isaac, Jacob, Moses, Aaron, Joseph, and David. When we complete our temporary sojourn on earth, the *ushpizin* will greet us as we enter our eternal home.

On Succos we also have the mitzvah of the four species: the *esrog* (citron), the *lulav* (palm tree branch), the *haddas* (myrtle), and the *aravah* (willow). The latter three are bound together, held with the *esrog*, and waved in the four directions as well as up and down.

Kabbalah states that these four species are unique because whereas supervision over all vegetation has been assigned to angels, these four species are under the direct supervision of Hashem. These four species, therefore, symbolize *hashgachah pratis*, Divine providence, that Hashem watches over everything. Inasmuch as no angel has access to these four species, they have the status of being the scepter of Hashem. Using the king's scepter is a capital offense, the only exception being the crown prince, the king's son. By holding these four species, Hashem's scepter, we indicate that we are His children.

Halachah states that a king is forbidden to forgive an offense against the crown. Inasmuch as Hashem is Sovereign of the Universe, and committing a sin is a defiance of His orders, how can He forgive our sins? The answer is that we are His children, and in the capacity of a father to a child, He can grant us forgiveness. This is why we address Hashem as *Avinu Malkeinu*, our

Father, our King. Hashem is indeed our King, but we also relate to Him as a child to a father. When we take the four species, which are "the Divine scepter," thereby indicating that as "princes," children of the King, we have a right to them, we validate the forgiveness that Hashem granted us on Yom Kippur.

Why wave the four species in six directions? The Talmud says that this is to dispel the "harmful spirits." We live in an environment where toxic spirits impact upon us from all sides. Our only defense against them is to reinforce our belief in *hashgachah pratis*, that we are at every moment under the watchful eyes of Hashem, and that He is in control of everything that may happen to us. In addition, as princes, our conduct should conform to our lofty status, as Hashem said to us at Sinai, "You shall be unto Me a kingdom of priests and a holy nation" (*Exodus* 19:6). Holding the Divine scepter should make us cognizant of who we are and how we must behave.

The Midrash says that there are "70 different interpretations to Torah" (*Osios D'R' Akiva*). One mitzvah can represent a broad spectrum of concepts. There is an additional meaning to the mitzvah of the four species.

The four species may be seen as corresponding to the human anatomy. The *esrog* represents the heart (emotion), the *lulav* represents the spinal column (action), the lenticular *haddas* represents the eye (vision), and the lips-shaped willow leaf represents the mouth (speech). The four species must all be present, and the absence of any one of them invalidates fulfillment of the mitzvah. A person must take care that he uses his vision, speech, emotions, and actions in a way that is compatible with Torah. One is not free to exclude speaking or listening to *lashon hara* from his observance of Torah. Nor may one look at forbidden things or harbor forbidden thoughts. Rejection of any one mitzvah is tantamount to rejection of the entire Torah (*Chullin* 5a).

Yet another interpretation. In Torah literature, taste is equated with Torah, the nutrient of the *neshamah*, and fragrance is associated with good deeds. Thus the *esrog*, which has both taste and fragrance, represents a person who has Torah knowledge and performance of good deeds. The *haddas*, which has fragrance but no taste, represents a person who does good deeds but has no Torah scholarship. The *lulav*, taken from the date palm whose fruits have a sweet taste, represents a person who has Torah knowledge but a paucity of good deeds. The *aravah* is insipid, with neither taste nor fragrance, and represents a person who has neither Torah knowledge nor good deeds.

One might think that a person who lacks both Torah knowledge and good deeds has little worth. The mitzvah of the four species teaches us that every individual has great value. The mitzvah is not fulfilled unless one has *all* four species. Absence of the insipid *aravah* invalidates performance of the mitzvah no less than absence of the succulent *esrog*. We dare not assign different values to people. Every person is indispensable.

On Succos when the Temple was standing, there was a special ritual, the libation of water on the Altar. The Talmud describes in great detail the joyous celebration of *Beis Hasho'eivah*, the fetching of the water (*Succah* 5b, 53b). The courtyard of the Temple was lit up with numerous torches, and the brightness illuminated all Jerusalem. Rabban Shimon ben Gamliel juggled eight lit torches. The celebration was so intense that they went without sleep throughout Succos.

In my other writings, I have repeatedly emphasized the importance of self-esteem, of having a true self-awareness, knowing all of one's character strengths. I have cited the words of *mussar* authorities, that self-esteem is not *ga'avah* (vanity). To the contrary, self-esteem is an essential component of humility. Rabbeinu Yonah says that *ga'avah* is actually an attempt to escape from feelings of inferiority. Nowhere is this as evident as in the statement of Hillel at the celebration of *Beis Hasho'eivah*: "If I am here, then all is here. If I am not here, then who is here?" The Talmud lauds Hillel's exceptional humility (*Shabbos* 30-31).

We can better understand Hillel's statement with the comment of the Rebbe of Kotzk. "If I am I because I am I and you are you because you are you, then I exist and you exist. However, if I am I *because* you are you, and you are you *because* I am I, then I do not exist and you do not exist." This is a profound psychological insight. A person whose identity is based on what others think of

16: Succos and the Four Species / 105

him does not have an identity of his own. He is a mere appendage of others, totally dependent on their opinion of him. Instead of doing what he knows to be right, he does what he thinks will gain him the approval of others. "If I am not here with a personal identity, then who is here?"

The participants of the celebration of *Beis Hasho'eivah* were "the pious and people of good deeds." Some said, "How fortunate we are that in our youth we did nothing that would cast shame on our later lives," and others said, "How fortunate we are that in our later lives we corrected the mistakes of our youth." Everyone had cause to rejoice.

The messages of *Beis Hasho'eivah* are adequate reason for simchah: self-esteem, and the knowledge that a person can always redeem oneself.

Succos concludes with Simchas Torah, when we celebrate the completion of the weekly Torah readings and immediately begin the Torah again, signifying that Torah is without an end. The only infinite being is Hashem, and this is, therefore, in keeping with the statement of the *Zohar* that the Torah and Hashem are one unity. As we learn Torah and integrate it into our lives, we are integrating Hashem. This intimate bond with Hashem is more than adequate reason for a joyous celebration.

Although one may not be a Torah scholar, everyone should rejoice on Simchas Torah. There is an anecdote about R' Naftali of Ropschitz, who saw a person who was not at all a Torah scholar celebrating Simchas Torah with much exuberance. "What are you celebrating?" R' Naftali asked. The man responded, "Rabbi, if my brother was marrying off a child, would I not dance at his simchah? I may not know much of Torah, but all Jews are brothers. Inasmuch as my Torah-scholar brothers are celebrating a simchah, I share in their joy." R' Naftali highly praised this man's insight.

Little wonder that the Torah gives particular importance to simchah on Succos. It is laden with reasons for joy.

17
Passover – A Prelude to Simchah

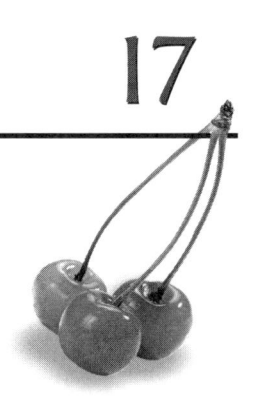

Many families gather together for the Passover Seder. They eat the matzah and the bitter herbs, drink the four cups, and recite the Haggadah. The house is free of all *chametz*. In our prayers we refer to Passover as "the festival of liberation." These are wonderful mitzvos. But, what do we take from Passover into our daily lives?

It should be obvious that Passover is more than a kind of Independence Day celebration. Who prepares for an Independence Day two weeks in advance, making the house *chametz*-free to a degree of operating-room sterility, replacing all dishes and cookware, and having a sharply restricted diet for eight days?

The deeper significance of Passover occurred to me when a

recovering drug addict told me that when his father began reciting the Haggadah at the Seder, and said, "*Avadim hayinu* (we were slaves)," he interrupted him. "Abba," he said, "can you truthfully say that you were a slave? Your ancestors were slaves, but you don't know what it means to be a slave. *I* can tell you what it is like to be a slave. All the years that I was on drugs, I had no freedom. I had to do whatever my addiction demanded. I did things that I never thought I was capable of doing, but I had no choice, no free will. I was the worst kind of slave."

This is a precious insight. Slavery is not limited to a despotic Pharaoh or a slave owner. A person can lose his freedom and be a slave to *himself,* to his habits and negative character traits. A person who cannot break free from cigarettes is a slave, as is someone who cannot break free from gambling, from excess food, from the Internet, and even from the office. A person whose self-concept is dependent on what others think of him, or whose behavior is totally determined by what he thinks others want him to be, he, too, has no freedom. He is not free to do what he thinks is right and proper, but what *others* think is right and proper. *Anytime one loses control of any aspect of one's behavior, one is a slave.*

I elaborated on this concept in the Haggadah, *From Bondage to Freedom*, showing how the entire Haggadah is essentially a text on breaking free from all forms of enslavement, internal as well as external.

This understanding of Passover and the Exodus explains why we have an entire week of celebrating independence. For political independence, one day of parades, picnics, and fireworks suffices. For the realization of obtaining true personal freedom, an entire week of contemplation is necessary.

Our susceptibility to being enslaved by our animalistic desires or by ego drives is so great that even a week's observance of the Exodus is not enough. We are subject to personal enslavement every day and many times during the day. That is why we have frequent reminders of the Exodus. Every Friday night in *Kiddush* we say that Shabbos is in commemoration of the Exodus. The daily mitzvos of *tefillin* and *tzitzis*, the blessing after meals, the redemption of the firstborn son, and even the avoidance of non-kosher species are reminders of the Exodus. Proper understanding of the significance of Passover and incorporating these principles in our daily lives can enable us to grow spiritually.

The centerpiece of Passover is, of course, the matzah. The *Zohar* refers to matzah as "the bread of faith." Presumably, this is because the Israelites left Egypt in such great haste that they could not take along any provisions, and took only the unleavened dough with them. With trust in Hashem they headed into the barren desert where no food was available. The matzah, therefore, represents the Israelites' faith and trust in Hashem.

Rabbi Zvi Elimelech of Dinov (*Bnei Yissaschar*) provides an additional insight. The prohibition of *chametz* on Passover is much harsher than that of other forbidden foods. For example, if a piece of *tereifah* meat falls into a pot of kosher food, and the volume of the kosher food is at least 60 times that of the *tereifah* meat, the food may be eaten. However, if a tiny crumb of *chametz* falls into a huge vat of food on Passover, even if the volume is infinitely great, 100,000,000 to 1, the entire vat of food is prohibited. The tiniest crumb of *chametz* cannot be considered negligible.

Bnei Yissaschar explains the difference between *chametz* and matzah. Matzah is never allowed to be left without someone working it. From the time the flour and water are combined, the dough is kneaded, promptly rolled out, perforated, and baked. Nothing happens to the matzah that is not the direct effect of someone handling it. Not so with *chametz*, where the ingredients are mixed and then set aside for a period of time to rise. The latter process is spontaneous, occurring without anyone's doing anything to make it rise.

Matzah and *chametz*, therefore, represent two perspectives. *Chametz* represents the idea that things can happen by themselves, while matzah symbolizes that nothing happens unless someone makes it happen. There is no spontaneity.

The Torah did not wish to deprive us of bread all year, but when we celebrate our independence and our free will, the matzah reminds us that there is no spontaneity in the world. Everything is at all times under the direct providence of Hashem. Except for the choice in behavior, of moral and ethical acts that Hashem assigned to man, there is not even the tiniest occurrence that is spontaneous. The Baal Shem Tov was very emphatic about this, saying that if someone digs into sand, each of the millions of grains of sand falls into the place where Hashem wills it to be. Not even the placement of a grain of sand is without design.

Matzah, therefore, symbolizes that everything in the world, great and small, is under the direction of Hashem. That is why the *Zohar* refers to matzah as "the bread of faith."

In the order of the Seder, we eat the matzah before the *marror* (bitter herbs). Inasmuch as the *marror* symbolizes the enslavement, would it not be proper that the *marror* precede the matzah, which represents the liberation? Herein lies an important concept. The Israelites had become so inured to being slaves that they did not recognize the bitterness of the condition. It was only after they had a taste of freedom that they realized how bitter it was to be a slave.

This can be applied directly to addiction. During the addiction, one is unaware of the brutality of his condition. It is only after one breaks free of the bonds of the addiction that he can understand how dreadful this condition had been.

But addiction is not the only time this phenomenon occurs. A person may be living a lifestyle in which he believes himself to be happy, and only when he is enlightened does he realize how mistaken he had been to think that he was truly happy. It is common for *baalei teshuvah* to report that prior to becoming observant of Torah, they had considered themselves to be happy. It was only after they discovered Torah that they realized how insipid their lives had been. True, there were no restrictions to their behavior and they could indulge in any pleasures they desired. In retrospect they see that a life without a higher goal, a life devoid of spirituality, is beneath the dignity of man. The spirituality in Yiddishkeit provides them with a simchah that had eluded them previously.

In ordaining the festival of Shavuos, the Torah says it should be celebrated with simchah. In the mitzvah of *succah*, the Torah mentions simchah three times. However, in regard to Passover, the Torah does not mention simchah at all. Why?

As noted, Passover represents independence. However, the emancipated Israelites had not yet received the Torah. They were indeed free in the sense that they no longer were slaves to Pharaoh, but they had no Torah, no sense of duty or responsibility. This kind of freedom results in the carelessness and recklessness of an untamed animal and this cannot be a state of simchah. It was only with the advent of Shavuos, with the giving of the Torah, that simchah was possible.

The conspicuous omission of simchah in the mitzvah of Passover is to impress upon us the teaching that true freedom requires adherence to Torah. Passover is, therefore, designated as a *prelude* to simchah, the simchah that is realized on Shavuos.

18
Counting of the Omer

On the second night of Passover, we begin the mitzvah of Counting of the *Omer*. When the Temple was intact, a barley offering of the new grain was brought on the second day of Passover ("*omer*" is a dry measure). Each night is counted: "Today is one day of the *Omer*, today is two days of the *Omer*, etc." Beginning with the seventh day, the counting is, "Today is seven days, which is one week of the *Omer*; today is eight days, which is one week and one day of the *Omer*, etc." Forty-nine days are counted, and the 50th day is Shavuos.

The *Omer* offering was the first mitzvah of the harvest. This was followed by the mitzvos of leaving the edge of the field uncut for the poor (*peah*), leaving stalks of grain that had fallen to the ground for the poor (*leket*), leaving a forgotten sheaf of grain for the poor (*shikchah*), and several tithes that were given when the harvest was complete. In addition to providing for the poor, these mitzvos reminded the farmer that the land belongs to Hashem, and that he works the land by the grace of Hashem.

Although we no longer have the Temple today, the sages ordained that we continue the practice of counting the *Omer*.

The kabbalists added to this ritual. They cite the seven affects: *chesed* (kindness), *gevurah* (strength), *tiferes* (splendor), *netzach* (triumph), *hod* (glory), *yesod* (foundation), and *malchus* (sovereignty). Each of these affects can be qualified by combining with the six others. Thus, there is *chesed she'bechesed* (intense kindness), *gevurah she'bechesed* (strength in kindness), etc. This results in 49 combinations, one for each day of the *Omer*. We pray that by fulfilling the mitzvah of counting the *Omer*, we will rectify any defects in our affective lives.

There is an extremely important teaching in the counting of the *Omer*. The many restrictions ordained by the Torah constitute a formidable challenge, as do the many positive mitzvos. The *yetzer hara* tells a person, "There is no way you can maintain so rigorous a conduct with so many deprivations and obligations for an entire lifetime. This is simply unrealistic, beyond a person's capacity. Inasmuch as this is impossible for the long term, why undertake something at which you are certain to fail?" By exaggerating the demands of living according to Torah law, the *yetzer hara* may entice a person to reject observance of Torah.

One can rebut the *yetzer hara* by saying, "I don't have to think about a lifelong commitment. I cannot do anything today about the challenges I will face next year, next week, or even tomorrow. The only thing I can do today is to deal with the challenges confronting me today, and it is certainly within my capacity to do so for one day." By taking one day at a time, complete Torah observance is feasible.

The method of taking "one day at a time" was adopted by Alcoholics Anonymous. It was recognized that a person who is totally dependent on alcohol cannot conceive living an entire lifetime without a drink. Inasmuch as this appears to be unrealistic, there is no point in trying to stay sober." Why engage in a futile pursuit? Don't torture yourself for no reason. Go ahead and have a drink now. The alcoholic is told, "You cannot do anything today about whether or not you will drink tomorrow, so why bother with it? Just stay sober today, and when tomorrow comes, you can worry about that then." A friend of mine wrote down in his calendar every day he was sober, The night before he died, he entered the number 15,736 in his calendar. He had been sober for 43 years, one day at a time.

A person may think, *How can I commit myself to never telling a lie?* That is unrealistic. Circumstances occur when one must lie. Or, *Never losing my temper, or never holding a grudge? I am not an angel!* That is unrealistic. Or, *Giving away one-tenth of my earnings to tzedakah every year? That will amount to a fortune!* These and other behaviors may appear to be formidable if one undertakes them for a lifetime.

The 49 days of the *Omer* culminate in Shavuos, when we celebrate receiving the Torah at Sinai. As a precursor to accepting the Torah, we count each day, and are reminded that each day we must deal with the challenges of that day, not those of the future. That is doable, and with that attitude, observance of Torah is well within one's means.

Conducting oneself according to refined character traits may be a challenge, and if one contemplates this for a lifetime, he may give up. The message of the counting of the *Omer* makes this challenge bite-size. It is obvious that observing this mitzvah contributes to character refinement.

During the days of the counting of the *Omer*, weddings are not performed and one may not take a haircut, restrictions that apply during mourning. The reason for this is that during this period, thousands of students of Rabbi Akiva perished. This was because "they did not show proper respect to one another" (*Yevamos* 62b).

The students of Rabbi Akiva were great Torah scholars, and if they were remiss in how they related to one another, it was only to their peers, not to their superiors. Nevertheless, they were punished so severely. The quasi-mourning period of the *Omer* should serve as a reminder of the enormous importance Torah gives to relating with great respect to every person.

By adopting the practical method of "one day at a time" and relating with due respect to everyone, we develop the character improvement that should enable us to have the simchah of self-fulfillment.

19

SHAVUOS AND THE TORAH

Shavuos is perhaps the most important of all the festivals. In contrast to Passover, which is characterized by the restriction of *chametz*, eating the matzah, and relating the story of the Exodus, and in contrast to Succos, which has the mitzvos of dwelling in the *succah* and the four species, Shavuos has no special mitzvah, other than abstinence from work. On Shavuos we do not focus on any one mitzvah, but rather on our receiving the Torah, which contains *all* the mitzvos.

The Torah reading on Shavuos is about the receiving of the Torah at Sinai, and the commentaries say that we should re-enact, in our imagination, the scene at Sinai: the mountain, covered by a cloud, aflame and trembling; the sound of the shofar;

Moses ascending the mountain; and three million people standing assembled at the bottom of the mountain, hearing the voice of Hashem saying, "I am your G-d." In recreating this scene, we are participating in the greatest moment in Jewish history.

Although the event at Sinai took place three thousand years ago, we should relive it on Shavuos. The blessing we recite on the Torah is "Blessed is Hashem, Who *gives* the Torah." We say "gives" rather than "gave" to stress that the Torah should be as exciting and fresh to us as though it was given to us just today. It is important that we keep the Torah fresh, to avoid our observance of mitzvos deteriorating into a habitual routine.

One might think that the refinement of character required by Torah is more than the average person can do, and as one reads the anecdotes about how our *tzaddikim* lived, one might say, "How can you expect this of me? I cannot be a Chafetz Chaim."

On Shavuos we read that prior to giving us the Torah, Hashem said, "You shall be to Me a kingdom of priests and a holy nation" (*Exodus* 19:6). Our great Torah personalities were not born as such. They were subject to the same desires, urges, and drives that we have. They struggled and made great effort to overcome the self-centered, self-gratifying tendencies inherent in human beings, and developed their character to the lofty spiritual levels they achieved. Our *tzaddikim* had no exclusive possession of this process. Rambam says that every person can become as great as Moses. "A kingdom of priests and a holy nation" means that every individual is capable of becoming priestly and holy.

The sages tell us that Hashem chose the mountain of Sinai as the site for giving the Torah because it is the lowest of the mountain range, to teach us that Torah can exist only when one humbles oneself. Humility is the *sine qua non* for proper Torah observance and character refinement.

Vanity, the antithesis of humility, is a barrier to Torah observance. Although Hashem says, "I will dwell with them even amid their contamination" (*Leviticus* 16:16), He nevertheless says, "A vain person and I cannot coexist in the same place" (*Arachin* 15b).

19: Shavuos and the Torah

In my writings, I have argued that contrary to what one might think, a vain person does not really think well of himself. Vanity is a desperate defense whereby one seeks to escape from the distressing feeling of unworthiness. I was thrilled to find this affirmed by the great ethicist, Rabbeinu Yonah. A person who has an inherent feeling of worthiness has no need to be vain.

Hashem's words before the giving of the Torah should dispel any feelings of unworthiness. "You have seen what I did to Egypt, and that I have borne you on the wings of eagles and brought you to Me. And now, if you hearken well to Me and observe My covenant, you shall be to Me the most beloved treasure of all peoples" (*Exodus* 19:4-5).

Every person should think of himself as a "beloved treasure," unique to Hashem. As such, one should refrain from any behavior that is beneath the dignity of someone who is a "beloved treasure" of Hashem, Reenacting the scene at Sinai should enable us to have the emotions of worthiness, sanctity, and humility, which will result in refinement of one's character.

King David says, "The Torah of Hashem is perfect, it restores the soul. The testimonies of Hashem are upright, gladdening the heart" (*Psalms* 19:8-9). R' Samson Raphael Hirsch comments, "Only by subordinating themselves to the will of Hashem can His creatures on earth become that which they should be and fulfill the purpose that gives meaning to their existence." In contrast to all other living things that function according to instinctual drives and hence cannot choose between good and evil, the human being is unique in having free choice. "Man has been ennobled by the will of Hashem, for He has implanted within him a spark of His own free personal Being."

Man has the capacity to follow his animalistic drives, which would then bring him down to an animal status, but the Torah enables man to rise above these. "I created the *yetzer hara,* and I created the Torah as its antidote" (*Kiddushin* 30b). R' Hirsch continues, "The laws of Hashem are in perfect accord with the nature and purpose of the creatures with which they deal and also with the nature and calling of ourselves, to whom they were given. Therefore, *they rejoice the heart.* There can be no substitute for this feeling of quiet joy and serenity, secure in the knowledge that we have done what was expected of us in life. For there is only one true joy, eternally bright. That is, the gladness that smiles upon us from every little plant, that shines forth from every one of our marvelous fellow-creatures — the joy that comes from a life of duty fulfilled, of consecration of all our desires and achievements to the fulfillment of the will of Hashem."

The Talmud says, "Beloved are the people of Israel, for a cherished jewel was given to them" (*Ethics of the Fathers* 3:18).

As was noted, the Torah does not ascribe simchah to Passover, but does so to Shavuos, because the Torah is the only source of true and enduring simchah.

20
Chanukah – The Light of Judaism

One of the most pleasant mitzvos is that of Chanukah. One sees the menorah in many windows. Chanukah songs are sung, Chanukah *gelt* and gifts are given to the children, *dreidel* is played, and *latkes* and doughnuts are enjoyed. Inasmuch as there are no work restrictions, people travel to share Chanukah with friends and family.

Chanukah celebrates the triumph of the Hasmoneans over the ruling Syrian-Greeks. In contrast to the domination of the Babylonians, the Greeks were not interested in physical persecution or destruction of the Jewish people. Their goal was to establish Hellenism as the state "religion." They did not destroy the Temple as did the Babylonians. Rather, they converted it to pagan worship.

The Greeks can be thought of as being "intoxicated" with the achievement of the human intellect. Strangely, it seems that the human mind lay dormant until the Age of Pericles, beginning in the fifth century B.C.E. There was an unprecedented "explosion" of intellectual achievement, beginning with the pre-Socratic philosophers, through Socrates, Plato, and the peripatetic school of Aristotle. Suddenly, people began investigating the world instead of taking it for granted. The intellectual achievements of these philosophers were hailed by no less an authority than Rambam.

I believe that what occurred at that point in history was similar to what we experienced in the 1960's, with the "G-d is dead" movement. The two decades preceding 1960 were extraordinarily productive in science, technology, and medicine. Miracle drugs saved lives that had previously been doomed; surgery progressed to correcting heart defects and replacing nonfunctioning organs; jet flight; space travel; television; computers, and countless other marvelous inventions testified to the genius of the human mind. Man's mind was supreme, and there was no longer any need for a "Supreme Being." The human intellect was thought to be capable of resolving any and all problems in the world.

I believe that the unprecedented intellectual achievement and knowledge of the world in the Age of Pericles was essentially a "G-d is dead" concept. The human mind was the measure of all things. Of course, the unaided human mind was free of all restrictions. Nothing was prohibited if it did not harm anyone. Social laws to protect a person's rights were all that was necessary. Pagan "religion" was ideal. The pagan gods were examples of the ultimate in self-gratification.

This concept was quite attractive to those Jews who wanted to be free of Torah restrictions, and they were only too happy to accept Hellenism. This, of course, would do away with observance of Shabbos, kashrus, *tefillin, tzitzis*, and the many other Torah laws. Relationships forbidden by the Torah were permissible. The attitude often espoused in the 21st century, "If it feels good, do it," was the consequence of Hellenism.

It is obvious that adoption of Hellenism amounted to total

rejection of Torah, and this is what the Hasmoneans fought. The military triumph of the Hasmoneans pales in comparison to their spiritual victory: the rejection of Hellenism and loyalty to Hashem and the Torah. It is the spiritual victory, symbolized by the Menorah miraculously burning for eight days with pure, uncontaminated oil that we primarily celebrate.

We have previously noted that character refinement requires mastery over one's animalistic desires and self-gratification. Hellenism was a repudiation of spirituality and the enthronement of the idea, "If it feels good, do it," a philosophy that reduces man to being nothing more than *homo sapiens,* an animal with intellect.

Lighting the Chanukah menorah is more than commemorating the miracle where a single vial of oil lasted for eight days. As with the Menorah in the Temple, the menorah we light represents the light of Hashem and that Torah illuminates our lives, as we say in our prayers, that Torah is *Toras chaim,* a Torah of life.

The Talmud says that the wicked are considered dead even during their lifetime *(Berachos* 18b). The human being is a composite entity, comprised of a physical body and a spirit. It is the spirit that distinguishes man from other living things. A person who is devoid of spirituality may indeed be alive, but it is only the physical, animal component that is living. As a unique human being, he is indeed lifeless. It is when we rise above physicality through Torah observance that we are fully alive as distinguished human beings.

The verse in the account of Creation reads, "The earth was astonishingly empty, with darkness upon the surface of the deep" *(Genesis* 1:2), upon which the sages comment, "darkness refers to the kingdom of Greece, for it darkened the eyes of Israel with its decrees" *(Bereishis Rabbah* 2:4). The Hellenistic concept of life extinguished the light of the human spirit, rendering man nothing more than an intellectual animal.

In the Chanukah liturgy, we say that the "lights of the Chanukah menorah are sacred. We may not utilize them for our own purposes. We may only look at them." To utilize their light, even to read, would be putting them to personal use, which is essentially self-gratifying, and this is the antithesis of the Chanukah lights.

There is certainly simchah in celebrating Chanukah with *dreidels*, Chanukah *gelt*, and *latkes*, but the most significant simchah of Chanukah is that the rededication of the Temple and the Menorah represented the triumph of spirituality over physicality.

21

PURIM – THE GREATEST MIRACLE?

The simchah of Purim hardly needs any commentary. It is clearly the most festive day of the year. Yet, the simchah of Purim is of even greater importance than most people think.

If one were asked, "What is the greatest miracle in Jewish history?" he would probably say, "The splitting of the Reed Sea." What can possibly equal the phenomenon of the waters of the sea dividing to allow the Israelites to pass through, and then closing again to drown the pursuing Egyptian army?

The chassidic writings give Purim extraordinary importance, and state that the miracle of Purim surpasses the miracles of Passover. Indeed, there is a Midrash that states that after Mashiach comes, the only Yom Tov that will be celebrated will be

Purim (*Midrash Mishlei* 9). (Torah commentaries struggle to explain this Midrash, which implies that all the other Festivals will no longer be observed. This is in contradiction to the principle that everything in Torah will continue eternally.) What is it that gives Purim such significance?

The miracles of Passover were supernatural. The laws of nature were suspended, the Reed Sea split apart, manna fell daily from heaven (a double portion on Friday), the Clouds of Glory surrounded the Israelites, and a pillar of cloud by day and a pillar of fire by night guided them in the desert for 40 years. There was no possible doubt that this was the direct work of Hashem. It is easy to recognize the work of Hashem in supernatural miracles. However, when things proceed naturally, we may tend to forget that Hashem is in control of everything. We may see rain as the natural culmination of the processes of evaporation and condensation. Both chassidic and *mussar* writings stress that "nature" is in reality a series of recurring miracles. This requires *emunah*.

There was nothing frankly supernatural on Purim, just a series of quite natural events. A drunken king flies into a rage and has the queen executed. She is replaced by Esther, a Jewess who keeps her ethnic identity a secret. An anti-Semitic prime minister plots to exterminate the Jews. The queen's uncle, Mordechai, discovers a palace intrigue to assassinate the king, saving the king's life. The king forces Haman, who wishes to kill Mordechai, to bestow honors on him. The queen reveals she is a Jewess, and pleads for her people. Haman is executed, and Mordechai becomes prime minister. The Jews are saved.

Not a miracle, right? Wrong! The series of "natural" events were orchestrated by G-d. Purim was no less of a miracle than the Exodus, but here the Hand of G-d was *concealed*. We believe that there are many "miracles" that we mistake as natural phenomena because the Hand of G-d is concealed.

The significance of Purim is that it teaches us the principle that Hashem is in charge of everything that happens in the world. All nature is the handiwork of Hashem, Who conducts the world with *hashgachah pratis*, Divine providence. The "natural" events of

Purim were no less miraculous than the dividing of the Reed Sea.

On Chanukah and Purim, we recite the *shehecheyanu berachah* thanking Hashem for "the miracles that He did for our ancestors, *in those days and in this time.*" This is understood to mean, "in those days," at the point in history when these miracles occurred, and "in this time," in this time of the year. An obvious question is: Why do we not recite this *berachah* on Passover, when there were so many wondrous miracles?

R' Levi Yitzchak of Berditchev points out that "time" is a concept within nature. Time does not relate to Hashem, because time is a measurement, and eternity is not subject to measurement. The miracles of Passover were supernatural, and inasmuch as they were not within nature, they were not within time. We do recite the *berachah* on Chanukah and Purim, because the epic of Purim, as noted, appeared to be a natural phenomenon, as did the victory of the Hasmoneans. Although the latter were outnumbered by the Greek army, it is not unnatural for guerrilla warfare to triumph even over a powerful army, hence these were miracles *"in this time."*

Disruptions of nature are one-time occurrences, whereas miracles occurring within nature are enduring. Purim reminds us of *hashgachah pratis*, that Hashem is always with us, even though His presence may be concealed. Indeed, some explain the custom of eating *kreplach* and *hamentaschen* on Purim, because the meat or the sweet jam fillings are enclosed, concealed as it were, in a wrapping of dough. This represents the miracles that were concealed under the cloak of nature.

There is an additional teaching of Purim. Mordechai and Esther established Purim to commemorate the salvation of the Jews from annihilation, and wished the festival to be an expression of gratitude to Hashem. However, we cannot give Hashem any gifts as a token of our thankfulness. Therefore, in keeping with the Baal Shem Tov's concept, that love of one's fellow Jew is the path to love of Hashem, they instituted the practice of giving to the needy and exchanging gifts with friends. Giving to Hashem's children is essentially giving to Him, and this is something we can do all year round.

The knowledge that Hashem is *always* with us is certainly reason for great simchah, and although the conviviality of Purim is celebrated only one day in the year, the message of Purim should give us much simchah all year round.

22
Rosh Chodesh (The New Month) — Renewal

The Jewish calendar is based on the phases of the moon, in contrast to the secular calendar, which is based on the sun. On the Shabbos before *Rosh Chodesh*, we say a prayer announcing the beginning of the next month. During the phase of increasing lunar light, we recite the prayer for. *Kiddush Levanah* (sanctification of the moon).

It is significant that the very first mitzvah Hashem commanded prior to the Exodus was establishing the lunar calendar. It is also noteworthy that when the Greeks tried to undermine Torah observance (prior to the Hashmonean revolt), they sought to suppress three mitzvos: Shabbos, *bris milah* (circumcision), and the lunar calendar.

Focusing on Shabbos and *bris milah* is understandable. These are two of the most fundamental mitzvos of the Torah. But in what way is the lunar calendar so important to Yiddishkeit that of all the 613 mitzvos, the Greeks singled out *Rosh Chodesh* for suppression?

In contrast to the sun, which is constant, the moon is cyclical, its light waxing and waning. This pattern corresponds to Jewish history. We have had times when we were at our zenith, and other times when we were at our nadir.

It is said that world history is characterized by the "rise and fall" of empires. This is not quite correct. Rather, it is the "rise and disappearance" of empires. Jewish history is markedly different. Greece once ruled the world, but Greek greatness is a thing of the past. The mighty Roman empire was thought to be indestructible, but walking on the remnants of Rome in the Forum, we see how it has crumbled into insignificance. In our own times, "the sun never set on the British empire," but that, too, is now relegated to history. No one expects that Greece, Rome, or Britain will ever return to their glory.

Not so with the Jewish nation. We face reality. We have had our highs and lows. When we are at the zenith, we do not get carried away, becoming vain and overbearing, and when we are at the nadir, we do not lose hope of a brighter future. We understand that our reality is cyclical, very much like the moon.

When the moon is ascending, we recite *Kiddush Levanah,* in which we say, "To the moon He (Hashem) said that it should renew itself as a crown of splendor for those borne (by Him) from the womb (the Jewish nation), *who are destined to renew themselves like it.*" In contrast to the mighty empires that exist only in archaeological findings, we hope for the return of Jewish majesty.

As our people was about to be forged into a nation, Hashem gave them the mitzvah of the lunar calendar, a symbolic lesson for coping with reality. When the Greeks overran Judah, they knew that as long as Jews hoped for a return of their greatness, they could not be vanquished. Decreeing discontinuance of the lunar calendar, eliminating their hope, was the Greek strategy for subduing the Jewish state.

This concept is as appropriate for the individual as it is for the nation. At the height of success, one should maintain humility, and in times of depression, one should not despair. The hope for renewal, for the individual and for the nation, enables us to have simchah under all circumstances.

23
TZITZIS —
THE THREADS
THAT BIND

As a result of being absorbed in daily activities, whether at work, in the home, or in social interaction, we are at risk of becoming so preoccupied that we may lose sight of our need for simchah at all times. The various mitzvos and the festivals indeed remind us of simchah, but in the interim we may lose sight of it. Indeed, the lure of the pleasures of the physical world are seductive; at any time we may be drawn to seek simchah in indulgence. The mitzvah of *tzitzis* serves as a constant reminder of our relationship to Hashem.

Indeed, the mitzvah of *tzitzis* was ordained for just this reason. The Torah relates that during the Israelites' sojourn in the desert, a man was discovered to be doing work on Shabbos. Moses said to Hashem that during the weekdays, the *tefillin* remind a person of his Torah obligations, but inasmuch as the *tefillin* are not worn on Shabbos, this person was forgetful of his Torah obligations. Hashem then prescribed the mitzvah of *tzitzis*, instructing us to put *tzitzis* on a four-cornered garment, so that when we see the *tzitzis* we will be reminded of all the mitzvos, and in particular, that we not go astray after the desires of our eyes and hearts (*Numbers* 15:38-40).

When we put on *tzitzis*, we say, "May it be Your will, Hashem, that the commandment of *tzitzis* be as worthy before You as if I had fulfilled it in all its details, implications, and intentions, as well as the 613 mitzvos that are dependent upon it." In what way are all the mitzvos of the Torah dependent on *tzitzis*?

The fact that the mitzvah of *tzitzis* is applied to a garment is significant. The function of clothing, in addition to providing warmth, is twofold. Clothing covers a person, thus concealing him, yet it is the way one presents himself to the world. A garment is thus symbolic of both our internal life and also of our relationship to others.

Our relationship to Hashem knows no boundaries. In our morning prayers we say, "Always let a person be G-d fearing privately and publicly." Our internal life, known only to us, must be every bit as devoted to Hashem as our external life.

A fragmented person cannot have simchah. *Tzitzis* represents the holistic perspective of Yidddishkeit.

There is a special halachah regarding *tzitzis* that conveys an important message. The Torah prohibits *shaatnez*, the intermixing of linen and wool fibers in a garment. However, if one has a linen garment, the Torah states that one may affix woolen *tzitzis*. Why this exception?

Although the mitzvah of *shaatnez* is a *chok*, an ordinance that has no apparent logical explanation, *Pirkei D'Rabbi Eliezer* (21) suggests that it contains an important teaching.

Whereas the first sin was that of Adam and Eve eating of the Tree of Knowledge, the first crime was Cain's murder of Abel. The Torah says that Cain was a "tiller of the ground" and Abel "became a shepherd" (*Genesis* 4:3). Cain became jealous when

Hashem accepted Abel's offering but rejected Cain's offering, and this envy led to Cain killing his brother. The first crime was the result of envy. Cain's remark, "Am I my brother's keeper?" indicated that he did not believe in Hashem's omniscience.

Wool, the product of sheep, is Abel's domain and linen (flax), a product of the ground, is that of Cain. We are restricted from mixing the two to remind us of the primordial fratricidal crime, so that we appreciate the destructiveness of envy.

Tzitizis, which bind us to Hashem, are a reminder of Hashem's omnipresence and providence. A person who has a trust in Hashem knows that Hashem provides his needs, and consequently will not be envious of what others may have. The principle of *tzitzis* is, therefore, the antidote to the sin symbolized by *shaatnez*.

An envious person cannot have simchah, because he is dissatisfied with his lot. Understanding the meaning of *tzitzis* can eliminate envy of others.

24

TEFILLIN — THOUGHT AND DEED

The *tefillin* contain parchments upon which are written the four sections of Torah where this mitzvah is prescribed. One of the pair of *tefillin* is worn on the arm and the other on the head.

The *kavannah* (intent) for *tefillin* is clearly stated in the introductory prayer to the mitzvah: "I intend with the putting on of the *tefillin* to fulfill the mitzvah of my Creator, Who has commanded us to put on the *tefillin* as is written in the Torah, 'and you shall bind them as a sign on your arm and let them be *tefillin* between your eyes' (*Deuteronomy* 6:8). These four portions (contained in the *tefillin*) declare His Oneness and Unity, so that we will recall the miracles and wonders that He did with us when He removed us from Egypt; and that He has the strength and dominion over those above and those below to do with them as He wishes. He has commanded us to put *tefillin* upon the arm to recall the 'outstretched arm' (of the Exodus) and that it be opposite the heart, thereby to subjugate the desires and thoughts of our heart to His service; and upon the head opposite the brain, so that the soul that is in my brain, together with my other senses and potentials may all be subjugated to His service."

The messages of *tefillin* are multiple. If we truly absorbed the message of the *tefillin*, "thereby to subjugate the desires and thoughts of our heart to His service... so that the soul that is in my brain, together with my other senses and potentials may all be subjugated to His service," we would reach the zenith of spirituality. The Talmud says that the verse, "Know Him in all your ways" (*Proverbs* 3:6), is "a small portion upon which the entire Torah is based" (*Berachos* 36a). The *tefillin* represent this fundamental concept.

Some people have an erroneous conception that there are phases of activity and behavior that belong to religion and others that are secular. Eating, sleeping, working and transacting, they feel, are beyond the scope of religion. The message of *tefillin* rejects this dichotomy. Our entire lives must be subjugated to the Divine will. Everything — one's thoughts, desires, and deeds — are all to be dedicated to the service of Hashem.

The order of putting on the *tefillin* is that the one on the arm is put on before the one on the hand. This represents the declaration of the Israelites at Sinai, "*naaseh venishma*" (we will do and we will obey; *Deuteronomy* 24:7). This is interpreted to mean that we will do whatever Hashem commands us, even if we do not understand the reason for the mitzvah. By putting on the arm-piece before the head-piece, we indicate that we are willing to follow the Divine commands, and that understanding them is not a prerequisite for performance. Furthermore, the Torah portions in the head-piece are on four separate parchments, whereas in the arm-piece they are on one parchment. In our minds we may have various opinions, but when it comes to action, we have only one goal: to obey the words of Hashem.

24: Tefillin — Thought and Deed

The *tefillin* are worn on the weaker hand (left arm in a right-handed person, right arm in a left-handed person) to remind us that it is not by the power of the hand that we achieve things. One of Moses' last teachings to the Israelites was, "You may say in your heart 'My strength and the might of my hand made me all this wealth!' Then you shall remember that it is Hashem Who gives you strength to make wealth" (*Deuteronomy* 8:17-18).

A person who trusts only in his own power cannot have peace of mind or simchah, because so many things are beyond one's control. The best-laid plans are frequently frustrated. A person who places his trust in Hashem knows that the all-powerful Being is looking after him and will see that his true, ultimate good is achieved.

The chassidic master, R' Zusia of Anipole, was always in a cheerful mood despite his abject poverty. Someone said to him, "How can you be so happy when your wife and children are miserable because they do not have the bare necessities of life?" R' Zusia answered, "How can they be happy? They put their trust in a ne'er-do-well like me. But I put my trust in the all-powerful G-d."

When we are totally devoted to Hashem and have trust in Him, we can have simchah.

> The following story was related to me by Yehoshua Hill, who heard it from Rabbi Yechiel Spero.
>
> Mordechai is a young man who volunteered in a nursing home. It occurred to him that some of the patients might want to put on *tefillin,* so he brought a pair and offered to help put them on. When he made this offer to Mr. G., the latter growled at him, "Get out of this room and don't you dare ever set foot here again!"
>
> Bothered by this apparently unreasonable outburst, Mordechai went back and said to Mr. G., "It's all right if you don't wish to put on *tefillin,* but what did I do wrong that you were so harsh toward me?"
>
> "What's your name?" Mr. G asked.

"Mordechai," he answered.

"Sit down there, Mordechai," Mr. G. said.

"I was 12 when my family was taken to Auschwitz. Everyone was killed except me and my father. On my 13th birthday, my father wanted me to put on *tefillin*. In our barracks, there was one man who had only a *shel yad* (the hand phylactery), but in another barracks, there was a man who had a pair. In the middle of the night, my father left the barracks, knowing he was risking his life. I stood looking out the fogged-up window anxiously, and my heart jumped when I saw my father coming. Suddenly a searchlight focused on him, and shots rang out. I ran toward him, shouting, 'Tattie, Tattie!' but he was gone. The Nazi soldier picked up the bag of *tefillin* and threw them at me. 'Take these if you want them!'

"I took the *tefillin* and looked up to the sky and said, 'I hate You, G-d! I hate You! My father risked his life so that I could put on *tefillin* on my Bar Mitzvah, and this is how You reward him? I swear, I will never put on *tefillin*, and no one else will ever put these *tefillin* on.' You understand, Mordechai? Now, get out of here."

As Mordechai was leaving, Mr. G. said, "Just open that dresser drawer." In the drawer was a pair of *tefillin*.

Weeks went by, and Mordechai never bothered Mr. G. again. One day, one of the patients told Mordechai that he has *yahrzeit* for his father and wants to say *Kaddish*, but they were able to assemble only nine men. With great trepidation, Mordechai went to Mr. G. "I know how you feel, but this man wants to say *Kaddish* on his father's *yahrzeit*. Could you please help make the *minyan*?"

Mr. G. hesitated for a moment, then said, "All right, but on one condition. I never want to see you again."

Several weeks later, when Mordechai got off the elevator, he saw Mr. G. sitting in his wheelchair, wearing the *tefillin*, adjusting the straps and mumbling something. Mordechai tiptoed behind him, and heard him saying tearfully, "Tattie, it feels so good! Tattie, it feels right!"

A few days later, Mordechai saw that the wheelchair was empty. Inquiring from the nurses, he learned that Mr. G. had just been taken to the hospital. Mordechai rushed to the hospital and was directed to Mr. G's room. A woman was standing outside the door. "He's gone," she said. "You know, all his life my father was depressed, full of fear and with frightening dreams. The past few days, he was calm. He died wearing the *tefillin*, and for the first time I can remember, he smiled.

"Would you happen to be Mordechai?' she asked. When Mordechai responded affirmatively, Mr. G.'s daughter said, "His last words were, 'Give the *tefillin* to Mordechai.' "

We can empathize with Mr. G., and I am sure that Hashem understood him. What we must understand is that while we assert our belief in Hashem every day with the *Shema,* Mr. G. expressed his belief in Hashem with his anger. Just reflect a moment. You cannot be angry at someone who does not exist. It was precisely *because Mr. G. believed in Hashem* that he was angry at Him.

The Talmud relates that Elisha ben Avuya, the teacher of Reb Meir, witnessed an incident that he felt was a gross injustice, and consequently became an apostate, denying the existence of G-d (*Kiddushin* 39b). Mr. G. did *not* deny the existence of G-d. To the contrary, he felt betrayed in the G-d he believed in, and was, therefore, angry at Him.

There are some people who believe in Hashem, but are not fully convinced about *hashgachah pratis,* that Hashem attends to every individual. Mr. G. did not consider his father's death an accident, but by blaming Hashem for it, he was asserting his belief that Hashem does attend to every individual. Hashem understood that Mr. G. had a full belief in Him, and He could wait for Mr. G's anger to play itself out.

The Talmud relates that Elazar ben Duradia was a profligate sinner all his life. As he was about to sin again, he heard a remark that electrified him, and he began to cry, repenting his sinful life and pleading for forgiveness. He wept uninterruptedly and died amid his weeping. A voice from heaven announced, "Rabbi Elazar ben Duradia has earned entrance into the Eternal World" (*Avodah Zarah* 17a). Elazar ben Duradia redeemed an entire lifetime of grave sins in his last moments, and not only earned entry into *Gan Eden*, but was also accorded the title "rabbi." Perhaps there was a voice from heaven when Mr. G. died, that he had earned entrance into *Gan Eden*.

The daughter said that before Mr. G. died, he smiled for the first time in years. He was wearing the *tefillin* that felt "so good." After so many years of anguish, he had a moment of simchah.

25
HONORING PARENTS

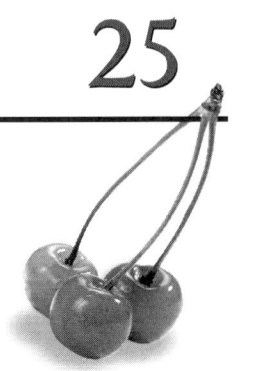

The importance of this mitzvah can be gathered from the Talmudic statement, "If a person honors one's father and mother, Hashem says, 'I consider it as though I was dwelling with them and they were honoring Me' " (*Kiddushin* 31a).

R' Shimon bar Yochai takes this one step further, saying that Hashem considers honoring one's parents to be a *greater* mitzvah than honoring Him. To prove his point, R' Shimon notes that the mitzvos of tithing are relevant only if a person has possessions, and that if a person cannot afford to buy *tefillin*, he is not obligated to beg for money. However, to provide for one's parents, a person must go begging if necessary (*Pesikta* 23).

The Midrash says that R' Yoshua was shown who his companion in *Gan Eden* will be. He went to meet the man, and when he asked the townsfolk about him, they said, "Why are you interested in him? He is a disgusting person." R' Yoshua asked the man about what mitzvos he did to deserve being his companion. The man answered, "I have an elderly father and mother. Every day, I bathe and dress them and feed them." R' Yoshua kissed the man and said, "How fortunate I am that I will have you as my companion in *Gan Eden.*"

The Torah requires both honoring and revering one's parents. Honoring them is defined by R' Yoshua's companion. Examples of reverence are that one speaks respectfully to them, does not contradict them, and does not sit in their place. If a parent commits a sin, one may not criticize him/her, but should say, "My dear parent, I think that the Torah says thus and so" (*Yoreh Deah* 240).

The Talmud cites a non-Jew as an example of honoring one's parents. Dama ben Nesinah had a gemstone needed for the *ephod* (breast-plate of the High Priest), and the Jewish elders were ready to buy it from him at a huge profit. However, his father was resting and the key to the safe was under his pillow. Dama refused to disturb his father's rest, despite having to forgo a huge profit. Hashem rewarded him. In the following year, a red heifer was born in his herd, and the sages were willing to pay an enormous sum for this rare animal, to fulfill the ritual of *parah adumah* (*Numbers* 19:1-22). Dama said, "I know you would pay me any amount I request. However, all I want is a sum equal to the profit I forwent when I did not sell you the gems" (*Kiddushin* 31a).

The Midrash relates another incident showing Dama's respect for his parents. Dama's mother was mentally ill, and when he was sitting with the notables of Rome, his mother beat him with her shoe. When she dropped the shoe, he picked it up and gave it to her (*Devarim Rabbah* 1). Another time she tore his garment and spit in his face, but he restrained himself and did not embarrass her (*Kiddushin* 31a).

This is the kind of *mesiras nefesh* that the mitzvah of honoring one's parents requires. "Dama was not obligated to observe the mitzvos of the Torah, yet he was so scrupulous in honoring his parents. We, who are obligated by the mitzvah, should be even more diligent in its observance" (ibid.).

The Talmud relates that R' Tarfon's mother lost her shoe, whereupon R' Tarfon put his hands beneath her feet so that she should not have to step on the cold earthen floor. When she praised her son to the sages, they said, "That is barely a beginning of fulfilling the mitzvah" (ibid.). R' Yosef, when he heard his mother approaching, said, "I must rise before the Divine Presence that accompanies her" (ibid.).

One must honor one's parents even after they are gone. If a person quotes something he heard from his father, he should say, "This is what my father, my teacher, said."

Adolescent psychologists report that the most frequent diagnosis they make is "Oppositional Defiant Disorder," wherein children rebel against their parents. Perhaps if these children had observed their parents' *mesiras nefesh* in honoring *their* parents, they would have behaved otherwise.

There is a story of a *tzaddik* who was accompanied by his disciples, and they heard shouting emanating from a house. They saw a man dragging his elderly father to throw him out of the house, and the father was pleading for mercy. The disciples were outraged, but could not do anything because the *tzaddik* was silent. When the man reached the threshold, the *tzaddik* ran in, seized him by his lapels and shook him vigorously. "You scoundrel!" he said, "How dare you mistreat your father this way!"

The disciples later asked him why he had restrained himself from reacting earlier. The *tzaddik* explained, "When this father was younger, he had tried to throw *his* father out of his house, but succeeded only in dragging him up to the threshold. Therefore, he deserved to be dragged up to the threshold, but not any farther."

How a person treats his parents serves as a model for how his children will treat him. Honoring one's parents provides not only the simchah of fulfilling this most important mitzvah, but also provides for greater simchah later in life, as one reaps the benefits of having taught one's children how to relate to parents.

26
The Chukim

*C*hukim are those Scriptural ordinances that are beyond our logical understanding. While we cannot claim to know the reason for *any* mitzvah, there are many mitzvos that are, to a greater or lesser degree, understandable. We can easily understand the prohibition of lying, stealing, and killing. We can even understand Shabbos as a vital day of rest. We can understand commemorating important historical events, and the appropriateness of respecting one's parents and being charitable to the needy. However, there are some laws that seem to have no logical explanation. A prime example is the prohibition of *shaatnez,* wearing a garment that has a mixture of linen and wool fibers.

In spite of some attempts to explain *shaatnez*, it remains a *chok*, an unsolved mystery.

This is equally true about many of the laws of kashrus. What is the reason that one may not mix meat with milk? Again, some attempts have been made to explain this, but it remains a *chok*. The prohibition of consuming blood and the meat of nonkosher animals has been explained as avoiding the negative effects these substances may have on one's emotions and judgment. In correspondence to a non-Jewish philosopher, Rambam says, "It is evident from your arguments that you have consumed meat from a predatory animal." This notwithstanding, we do not observe kosher laws because of psychological or physical health considerations, but because Hashem commanded them, and they are essentially *chukim*.

If *chukim* cannot be understood logically, how can they effect character refinement and how can they contribute to simchah? This requires our faith and trust in Hashem. One thing is beyond doubt: the *chukim* were *not* ordained to benefit Hashem. Hashem is all perfect and not in need of anything. Our only conclusion is that somehow observance of these *chukim* leads to our betterment in ways that we are unable to understand.

Acceptance of this should not be all that difficult. We submit to medical treatment, ingesting potent chemicals and undergoing mutilating surgery because we have trust that the doctor knows that these treatments are to our advantage. We do not understand nor is there a need for us to understand the mechanism whereby antibiotics destroy bacteria. It is enough for us that the doctor understands this, and we benefit from the antibiotic even though we do not understand how they work. If we have faith and trust in Hashem, we do not need to understand in what way the *chukim* are beneficial.

The very fact that we do not understand *chukim* has a very important benefit: *their observance indicates our willingness to submit to authority.* This is so vital in an era where Oppositional Defiant Disorder is the most common diagnosis given by psychiatrists and psychologists who treat adolescent disorders.

The 1960's were a watershed, introducing an era of loss of

respect for authority. The respect for teachers, religious leaders, and courts dwindled. Youngsters, who naturally strive for independence, picked up on this and defied parental authority.

Children are not likely to do what they are told, but are much more likely to emulate their parents and do as they do. It is, therefore, extremely important that parents demonstrate respect for authority.

Even in fully observant homes, such demonstration may be lacking. Rashi (*Leviticus* 20:26) cites the Talmudic statement that a person should not say, "I despise pork," but rather, "I would like to eat pork, but I do not do so because my Heavenly Father forbids it." The fact is, however, that for observant Jews, pork is an abomination, and one has no desire for it. Similarly, an observant Jew cannot say, "I would like to work on Shabbos, but I cannot because Hashem forbids it." Working on Shabbos is simply unthinkable. Showing respect for authority requires that we desist from something which we would like to do.

This is the benefit of the *chukim*. When parents take their garments to be checked for *shaatnez*, they can truthfully say, "I do not have the slightest idea why I cannot wear a garment that has *shaatnez*. I oberve this only because the Torah requires it."

If we demonstrate acceptance of authority, complying with laws that we do not understand, and make this clear to our children, there is greater likelihood that our children will emulate us and accept authority. Observing the *chukim,* precisely because we do not understand them, can, therefore, result in simchah. We can rest assured that just as a child does not understand the logic and benefit of obeying his parents, he nevertheless knows that they have his best interests at heart, likewise our observing the *chukim,* albeit without any concrete understanding of their necessity, provides us with the confidence that since we are obeying the will of Hashem, our Heavenly Father, this is in our best interests and the knowledge should result in simchah.

27
BRIS MILAH (CIRCUMCISION)

"When Abram was ninety-nine years old, Hashem appeared to Abram and said to him, 'I am El Shaddai; walk before Me and be perfect' "(*Genesis* 17:1). The patriarch was then given the mitzvah of *milah*, which is the eternal covenant between Jew and Hashem. *Milah* has thus been a basic precept of Yiddishkeit, and when anti-Semitic laws sought to prohibit *milah*, people were prepared to sacrifice their very lives for this mitzvah.

As was noted earlier, no one can claim to know the reasons for mitzvos. We observe them because Hashem commanded them. Although we may recognize all of the benefits derived from mitzvos, these are not the reasons we observe them, and if there are no discernible benefits, we observe the mitzvos anyway.

Claims have been made that there are health benefits from circumcision, and some have refuted these claims. This has no bearing on the mitzvah.

An interesting finding was made by my teacher, Professor Armand Quick, which he describes in his book, *Hemorrhagic Diseases*, and that is that vitamin K, one of the factors essential for blood clotting, does not appear in the newborn's blood *until the eighth day*!

Some ask: Why did Hashem not simply create infants in a circumcised state?

When Hashem created other forms of life, He created them in a state of completion. A newborn bear needs only to grow. It is endowed with all the qualities that make him a bear. He does not have to make any change, to transform itself into something other than what it was created. This is true of all living things, except man.

As I pointed out earlier, it was the Divine will to create a being that is not complete at birth, that is essentially raw potential, and that must develop himself to becoming a spiritual being. Man at birth is essentially animal in nature, totally self-centered. If a person does not develop proper character traits, he remains essentially an animal, albeit with greater intellect than other animals. Man must perfect himself through his own effort.

In commanding the mitzvah of *bris milah,* Hashem said to Abraham, "walk before Me and be perfect." Abraham was to understand that he was in a state of imperfection, and that becoming perfect is his responsibility, not that of Hashem. Just as man must perfect himself physically with circumcision, so must one perfect himself spiritually by his own effort. This mitzvah was given to the children of Abraham to make them distinct among all the peoples of the world.

At the *bris milah*, the infant is blessed, "Just as he entered into the covenant of *bris milah,*so shall he enter to the study of Torah, marriage, and good deeds." This blessing is unique to this mitzvah, and is not said at the performance of any other mitzvah.

Although the father arranges for the mitzvah to be performed, the child is the bearer of this mitzvah, a mitzvah in whose performance the infant could have no ulterior motive. The blessing is that when he studies Torah, marries, and performs good deeds, these, too, should be as free of ulterior motives as the *bris milah*, and should be performed solely in obedience to the will of Hashem.

The Talmud cites the verse in *Psalms* (119:162), "I rejoice over Your word, like one who finds abundant spoils," and states that the "word" King David is referring to is the commandment of circumcision. The Talmud adds that a mitzvah that Jews accepted with joy continues to be celebrated with great joy. We celebrate *bris milah* with a *seudas mitzvah,* a festive meal.

Chassidic masters insisted that there be a festive meal to celebrate *bris milah*, and if a family could not afford it, a collection would be taken up to finance it. They explained, "When Satan brings harsh charges against the Jews that they commit sins, the Archangel Michael says, 'Even so, their hearts are not in it. No one celebrates a sin. When they do the mitzvah of *bris milah*, they celebrate with a festive meal. Have you ever seen anyone celebrate a sin by calling friends and relatives to a festive meal?' Therefore, the festive meal is an integral part of the mitzvah."

Historically, anti-Semitic decrees always forbade circumcision. This was true under the oppression of the Syrian Greeks (the Chanukah story), and most recently under Communist Russia. Our enemies knew that *bris milah* is the foundation of Yiddishkeit.

Just a few years ago, a Russian immigrant in the United States announced in the shul the birth of a son, and that the *bris milah* would be in the shul at Tuesday, 10 a.m. He then went to each worshipper and whispered, "The *bris milah* will be at my home at 8 a.m." He explained that this is how it was announced in Russia. Because the Communists forbade circumcision, the public announcement was intentionally wrong, so that if the KGB came to shul at 10 a.m. they would find it empty. Although he was now in the United States, he still announced it as they did in Russia!

When such decrees were issued, Jews defied them, often at the cost of imprisonment or even death.

A survivor of Auschwitz told me that he identified with King David, of whom the Talmud says that when he had nothing else with him, and was in a place where he was not allowed to think about Torah, he rejoiced that he still had the mitzvah of *bris milah*. "That is how I felt when the Nazis took everything from me. I was enheartened that I still had the mitzvah of *bris milah*."

As David says, the simchah of *bris milah* is great indeed.

28

Pidyon Haben (Redemption of the First-Born Son)

This is one of the mitzvos whose reason is clearly stated in the Torah. "And it happened when Pharaoh stubbornly refused to send us out, that Hashem killed all the firstborn in the land of Egypt, from the firstborn of man to the firstborn of beast. Therefore, I offer to Hashem all male first issue of the womb, and I shall redeem all the firstborn of my sons" (*Exodus* 13:15). *Pidyon haben* is thus one of the ways we commemorate the Exodus.

According to the *Chinuch*, *pidyon haben* is similar to the tithes of *terumah*, the first tithe of the harvest; *bikkurim*, the offering of the first-ripened fruits; and *challah*, a tithe of the dough taken even before the bread is baked. All of these are "firsts," and are an expression of our awareness that everything in the world belongs to Hashem, and He has "first rights" to everything. We "redeem" the firstborn son, acknowledging that he is a gift that Hashem has given to us.

However, this does not explain why the mitzvah does not apply to a firstborn daughter, particularly since one Midrash says that the plague of the firstborn affected female firstborn as well as males. The reason firstborn daughters are exempt is because the redemption serves yet another purpose.

Prior to the sin of the Golden Calf, the priestly functions were carried out by the firstborn son (*Bamidbar Rabbah* 4:4). Jacob's acquiring the birthright from Esau was because Esau was unfit to do the Divine service. The only tribe that was not at all involved in the worship of the Golden Calf was the tribe of Levi. The priestly functions were then transferred from the firstborn to the tribe of Levi (*Numbers* 3:41), and the firstborn were "redeemed." Inasmuch as the priestly functions are performed only by males, firstborn daughters do not require redemption.

The firstborn son is redeemed with five *shekalim*. The Midrash states that the "twenty pieces of silver" for which the brothers sold Joseph (the firstborn son of Rachel) into slavery is equal to five *shekalim* (*Bereishis Rabbah* 84:17). The *pidyon haben* is thus a reminder of the sin of the brothers.

According to the latter, *pidyon haben* is a reminder of the far-reaching evil of envy, which can cause a fraternal hatred so great that it could result in selling a brother into slavery. *Pidyon haben* reminds us that we must uproot every trace of envy, and *pidyon haben* is also an acknowledgment that our children are Divine gifts, and we must care for them as such.

It is customary to celebrate *pidyon haben* with a festive meal, just as for *bris milah*. In addition to celebrating the mitzvah, it is also an expression of gratitude, because according to halachah, an infant is not considered viable until its 30th day, which is when one performs the *pidyon haben*.

There is special significance to the festive meal of *pidyon haben*. Tradition has it that a person who participates in the celebration of *pidyon haben* has merits as though he had fasted for 84 days! That is certainly cause for simchah!

29
Marriage and Family

"Hashem blessed them (man and woman) and Hashem said to them, 'Be fruitful and multiply' " (*Genesis* 1:28). Although the commandment appears to have been given to both man and woman, the Talmud derives that marriage and having children is a Scriptural obligation only of man. However, there is a prophetically based mitzvah for the woman as well.

The Torah states that "it is not good for man to be alone" (*Genesis* 2:18), and this holds true for the woman as well. The Talmud states that a person without a mate is only a "half person," bereft of good, of joy, and of blessing (*Yevamos* 62b).

A happy family life begins with the choice of a mate. The Talmud says that one should choose a mate with fine *middos*, and not for ulterior motives, such as money (*Kiddushin* 70a). "One should choose a wife who is appropriate for him" (ibid.).

"Appropriate" requires making a judgment. It requires knowing one's own character, aspirations, and goals in life and, as much as one can, that of a proposed spouse. Not infrequently, however, a person's judgment is affected by ulterior motives, such as physical attraction.

Why is physical attraction an ulterior motive? Because the goal in marriage should be to have a peaceful, harmonious, and happy relationship, where both partners share similar ideals and principles. This will minimize the conflicts that may threaten the solidarity of a marriage, and will enable both parents to teach and guide the children in a wholesome manner. Physical beauty, while understandably desirable, contributes little to this goal. It is natural for the intensity of physical attraction to wane, and if there are significant differences in the couples' ideals that are overlooked because of passion, these can become the cause of friction. A marriage that is fraught with dissension is one in which children may feel insecure, and the negative consequences of an unstable marriage on the children are legion. It has been well said that "the greatest gift that you can give your children is the love that you give your spouse."

Every mitzvah has its halachos, and marriage is no exception. Halachah prescribes how a husband and wife should relate to each other, with the utmost respect and consideration. The Talmud repeatedly condemns displays of rage within the home. "The reason I merited longevity is because I never raised my voice in my home." A person cannot be considered Torah observant if one violates the halachos of relating to one's spouse.

At the marriage ceremony, the couple is blessed with simchah. "Gladden the beloved companions as You gladdened Your creation in the Garden of Eden from aforetime. Blessed are You, Hashem, Who gladdens groom and bride." Adam was alone and lonely, and Hashem gladdened him with Eve.

Everything in the Garden of Eden was perfect, except that Adam was "bereft of good." Husband and wife should recognize that each one constitutes the "good" for the other.

Hashem indeed blesses the couple with simchah, but the Talmud says that "Hashem did not find a receptacle capable of receiving His blessings other than *shalom*" (end of *Uktzin*). When husband and wife relate in a manner that their home is a place of *shalom*, they merit the Divine blessing of simchah.

There is nothing that is of greater importance in Yiddishkeit than *shalom bayis*. The *Shechinah* (Divine Presence) rests in a home where there is *shalom bayis*, and where there is the *Shechinah*, there is simchah. Of course, there may be differences of opinion between a husband and wife, but a concerted effort should be made to resolve these in a way that *shalom bayis* is preserved. With mutual respect, tolerance, patience, and empathy, there can be eternal true love and simchah.

30
EMUNAH (FAITH)

The Chafetz Chaim describes the mitzvah of *emunah* as follows:

"It is a positive commandment to believe that there is a G-d in existence, as Scripture states, 'I am Hashem, your G-d, etc.' (*Exodus* 20:2); and He — may He be blessed and exalted — brought all existing entities into being, and all the worlds, by His power and blessed wish. It is He Who watches over everything. This is the foundation of our faith"(*The Concise Book of Mitzvoth*).

Torah writings are replete with the discussion as to whether one should accept belief in Hashem with pure, simple faith, or whether one should reason logically to the conclusion of the existence of Hashem. The consensus is that one should accept the existence of G-d on the uninterrupted transmission from Sinai, where some three million people heard the voice of Hashem saying, "I am Hashem, your G-d, Who delivered you from the land of Egypt." Once one has a firm faith, he may reason logically to reinforce his belief.

The validity of this position should be obvious. One does not need to believe in something that can be proven. That combining oxygen and hydrogen results in water can be demonstrated in the laboratory, as can the fact that 2 + 2 = 4. One does not have to *believe* these concepts. Belief is necessary only when something can *not* be proven.

There are a number of philosophical arguments for the existence of G-d, but all can be rebutted. Furthermore, human reasoning is fallible and is subject to a plethora of influences that may distort one's thinking.

Scripture relates the indulgence of Israelites in idolatry (*avodah zarah*). This is a phenomenon that is mind boggling. Jews are by nature skeptic. Even after witnessing miracle after miracle, culminating in the splitting of the Reed Sea, the generation of the Exodus was still unsure of Hashem. Are we to believe that Jews could possibly believe that an idol was a god?

The Talmud resolves this problem. "The Jews knew very well that the idols were worthless. They embraced idolatry only because they wanted a religion that would sanction relationships that the Torah forbade" (*Sanhedrin* 63a). Their desire to gratify their urges was so intense that it distorted their reasoning power, leading them to lose faith in Hashem.

Earlier it was noted that several attempts were made to encapsulate the Torah, and that ultimately, the prophet Habbakuk condensed the Torah into a single statement: "The righteous shall live by faith" (2:4).

Observance of the Torah is impossible as long as a person is dominated by self-gratification. As with the indulgence in idolatry, one can rationalize to whatever conclusions he desires, and one can easily deceive himself and believe himself to be righteous.

Avodah zarah is not restricted to idol worship. Any time one manipulates religion to conform to one's personal desires, that is *avodah zarah*. Habbakuk's statement is, therefore, that one can be truly righteous only on the basis of one's faith, not of one's logic.

Faith is confronted with many challenges. We believe G-d to be just, yet there are so many things that appear to us to be grossly unjust. Why do the innocent suffer? Where was G-d during the Holocaust?

There are no answers to these questions. When Moses asked Hashem why the innocent suffer, Hashem told him that this cannot be understood as long as one inhabits a human body. Yet, before he died, even though he was refused his most fervent wish to enter the Promised Land, Moses stated, "The Rock! — perfect is His work, for all His paths are justice" (*Deuteronomy* 32:4).

Our history is star studded with geniuses, some of whom were close enough to our own time that we have eye-witness testimony to their enormous intellect. The Chafetz Chaim totally effaced himself before the Gaon of Vilna, who, in turn, totally effaced himself before Rambam. These and many hundreds of super-minds thought of all the challenges to faith in Hashem that we can think of, yet they were firm in their belief in Hashem. Would it not be the height of arrogance if I were to consider my reasoning ability to be greater than theirs?

We cannot avoid having questions about *emunah*, and that is why we must renew our *emunah* every day, as we recite the *Shema* and declare that "Hashem, our G-d, Hashem is One." If *emunah* was not subject to challenges, there would be no need for renewing it every day.

With sincere *emunah*, we can overcome our innate self-centered drives. We can be considerate of others and make sacrifices to help others. We can conceive of a goal in life other than satisfying our egos and physical urges. We can develop mastery over our anger. In short, *emunah* enables us to develop refined character traits that give us the dignity of being man.

As was pointed out earlier, one of the definitions of simchah is *lev shalem*, "with a complete heart," and an unfaltering trust in Hashem. This is not the kind of simchah that is spontaneous, but one that requires dedicated effort, as is written, *Ivdu es Hashem besimchah*, "work toward serving Hashem with simchah."

31

THE HUMAN BEING — A SPEAKING SOUL

How often do we regret something we said, whether in anger, as gossip, or in haste? Unfortunately, our words cannot be retracted, and we may lose simchah because of unwise things we may say.

"And He breathed into his nostrils the soul of life, and man became a living soul" (*Genesis* 2:7). Onkeles translates the latter phrase as "a *speaking* soul," meaning that the distinctive feature of man that separates him from other living things is that man can communicate by speech. This unique ability that gives a human being his identity should be assiduously guarded.

The Talmud considers any violation of the halachos of speech as being extremely grave. The outstanding sage of the previous generation, the Chafetz Chaim, dedicated his life's work to the purification of speech, and his *sefer, Shemiras Halashon* (Guarding Speech), is not only mandatory reading for every person, but must be reread periodically. We engage in speech during much of our waking life, and unless we are extremely watchful, we may transgress some of the most serious prohibitions of the Torah.

It is self-evident that observing the halachos governing speech results in character refinement. However, because of the extreme vulnerability to abuse the gift of speech, we will follow in the path of the Chafetz Chaim to emphasize the importance of vigilance.

The Midrash says that *lashon hara* is destructive to three people: the speaker, the listener, and the object of the speech (*Devarim Rabbah* 8:10). The Talmud categorizes *lashon hara* as being equivalent to the three cardinal sins: idolatry, adultery, and murder (*Arachin* 15b). Rambam says that one who speaks *lashon hara* does not merit seeing the glory of Hashem in the eternal world. *Sefer Chassidim* says that on Judgment Day, a person may find himself charged with sins that he never committed. He is told, "These sins were committed by a person about whom you spoke *lashon hara*, and his sins were transferred to you."

In addition to the sin of *lashon hara,* one is also in violation of *lifnei iver* (causing another person to sin), because one who listens to *lashon hara* is also guilty of the sin. Similarly, one who listens to *lashon hara* is also in violation of *lifnei iver,* because without a receptive listener, the *lashon hara* would not have been spoken.

What kind of gratification is there that causes a person to speak *lashon hara*? I believe that by degrading another person, one has a feeling of superiority, that he is in this particular respect better than the other person. Seen this way, speaking *lashon hara* indicates that one has low self-esteem and resorts to *lashon hara* to relieve his feelings of inferiority.

R' Shlomo Zalman Auerbach noted that one is prone to listen to *lashon hara* about a person who lied, cheated, or misbehaved, but one is less interested to hear *lashon hara* about a murderer. This is because a person is comforted when he hears that others have the same character defects as himself. Inasmuch as one is not a murderer, one does not gain anything by hearing *lashon hara* about a killer. This should put a person on the alert. Listening to *lashon hara* about someone is essentially a public confession that one shares the guilt.

One Shabbos, the Chafetz Chaim lodged at an inn, and the innkeeper, not knowing his identity, seated him at a table with several other guests who were horse traders. At every meal, the conversation was about horses. After Shabbos, someone informed the innkeeper of the identity of this guest. The innkeeper apologized to the Chafetz Chaim for having exposed him to such unrefined company. The Chafetz Chaim, "To the contrary, I was very pleased to sit with them. You see, they spoke only about horses, not about people!"

While one can do *teshuvah* for most sins, it is more difficult to do *teshuvah* for *lashon hara*. If one shakes loose the feathers of a pillow, it is very difficult to retrieve them. So it is with *lashon hara*. Once defamatory remarks have been made about someone, it is virtually impossible to retrieve and undo them.

Another aspect of speech that the Torah stresses is *truth*. For no other transgression does the Torah require precautionary steps, but in regard to lying the Torah says, *"Distance yourself from a false word"* (Exodus 23:7). The Torah reinforces the prohibition of lying by requiring that a person avoid doing anything that may possibly lead to lying. This can be a golden rule for human behavior: "If you think that at some time you may have to deny having done something, *do not do it!*" This constitutes "distancing" oneself from a false word. Observing this dictum can eliminate many problems, and is a major contribution to character refinement.

Harav Kahaneman, Rosh Yeshivah of Ponivehz, related that the Chafetz Chaim once sent for him and said, "I have just sold a number of my *sefarim* and I have some money. Some people who ask me to lend them money are completely untrustworthy, and never repay a loan. One is not obligated to lend money to dishonest people. However, I cannot tell them that I do not have any money, because that is a lie. Therefore, I want to give you all my money as a gift with a binding act of transaction, so when I say that I do not have any money, I will not be lying."

R' Yechezkel Levenstein of the Mir yeshivah was a close friend and admirer of R' Yitzchok Sher. When the latter died, it was assumed that R' Levenstein would eulogize him, but to everyone's astonishment, he refused. He later explained, "Just recently I lost a dear grandchild. I felt that in my eulogy I might be overcome with the grief over my grandchild, and I might cry. The audience would think that I am crying because of the death of R' Sher, and I would be guilty of giving a false impression."

In pursuit of truth, a person should not deceive himself. A person should realize that rationalizing and explaining away his behavior is essentially lying, if only to himself. Absolute honesty is the crown of character refinement.

Another important aspect of speech is keeping one's word. "Whatever has passed your lips you shall keep and do, as you have vowed" (*Deuteronomy* 23:24).

Words should not be treated lightly. If one says, "I promise I'll return it tomorrow," and then delays returning it, one has transgressed this mitzvah. Sometimes one says, "I swear that I did it," or "So help me G-d." These are vows and must be taken very seriously. The Talmud says that when Hashem said, "You shall not take the Name of Hashem, your G-d, in vain" (*Exodus* 20:7), the earth trembled.

Our *gedolim* cautioned that one must be careful when promising something to a child. Sometimes one may entice a child to do something or to refrain from doing something by saying, "I'll give you something" or "I'll take you somewhere." Failure to keep a promise, even to a child, is a transgression. Furthermore, it teaches a child to be dishonest.

Meaningful relationships are built on trust. If one fails to keep a promise, one undermines the quality of the relationship, whether with a family member or a stranger.

I would like to elaborate on the latter point. Early in my psychiatric training, I had a patient who was a hypochondriac, constantly complaining of various aches and pains. I was certain that he was simply trying to obtain pain-relieving medication, and that he really was not in pain. I told the nurse to give him a placebo, which is an inert pill or injection that contains no medication at all. I was surprised when the nurse said, "Our policy is not to give placebos," because during my internship in general medicine we did use placebos.

Upon my inquiry for the reason for this policy, the director of the department said, "Words are not the only means of communication. We communicate by body language as well as verbally. While you can control what you say, you have little control over your body language. If you give a patient a placebo, your verbal communication is, 'I am giving you something,' but your body language will say, 'I am giving you nothing.' Your patient will get both messages, and he will lose trust in you."

I must admit that prior to this, I probably did my share of "justified" lying, i.e., white lies or *lemaan hashalom*, to preserve peace. With this insight, I have refrained from lying for one simple reason: *I am not a good liar!*

The events of recent years have proven the value of truthfulness. One president of the United States was toppled from office because of his attempt to cover up a bungled break-in, and another president humiliated his office by improper behavior and neared impeachment because he lied. I am convinced that truthfulness, even if temporaily costly, in the long run is conducive to simchah.

32
BERACHOS (BLESSINGS)

E arlier it was noted that there are *berachos* that one recites before doing a mitzvah, and there are *berachos* before partaking of anything. *Berachos* are an expression of willingness to fulfill the mitzvos, or an expression of gratitude for what Hashem has given us.

There are a broad spectrum of *berachos* for many daily activities. Upon arising in the morning, there is a *berachah* thanking Hashem for giving us another day of life. There are *berachos* of gratitude for the ability to see and walk, for having clothes and shoes to wear, and for having the energy to function. These *berachos* should make one aware that all these faculties are gifts from Hashem and should not be taken for granted. Furthermore, they are not outright gifts, but rather loans. At some time in our future these will be taken from us.

Teshuvah requires *vidui* (confession of one's sins). It is of interest that the Torah mentions *vidui* in regard to the sin of theft (*Numbers* 5:6-7). R' Yitzchak Meir of Gur explains why the Torah chose this sin to establish the requirement for confession.

If someone borrows an item for a specific use, he is not permitted to put it to any other use. For example, if he borrows an axe for the specific purpose of chopping wood, and then uses it as a digging tool, he is liable for any damage sustained by the digging, because it was an unauthorized use. In halachah, unauthorized use of something belonging to another individual is considered theft.

Hashem gives us a number of faculties that we are to use doing things that are mitzvos or permissible acts. Using any of our faculties for forbidden acts is an authorized use, hence it is theft. Eating nonkosher foods or speaking *lashan hara* is unauthorized use of the mouth, and doing a forbidden act on Shabbos is an unauthorized use of one's hands; hence these are forms of theft as well as sins on their own. The Torah, therefore, states the requirement for confession at the sin of theft, because every transgression is a form of theft.

When we say the *berachah* thanking Hashem for the gift of vision, we should reflect that He gave us this precious ability so that we may use it in His service, which we can do in many ways. However, if we look at things that are inappropriate, we are misusing this faculty, and this constitutes a kind of theft. This holds true for all other faculties that Hashem gave us.

There is a *berachah* we say for our personal needs. Again, we may take this for granted, and we may not be aware of it unless it does function well

When my father was a patient at the Mayo Clinic, a man who was there for treatment of a prostate problem said to him, "Rabbi, I don't understand why on Yom Kippur people put on a *tallis* and *kittel* for *Kol Nidrei*, and recite the prayers with great solemnity. Let me tell you, Rabbi, that when a person has taken care of his personal needs without difficulty, *that* is when he should put on a *tallis* and *kittel* and recite the *asher yatzar berachah* with great solemnity, expressing his profound gratitude toward Hashem."

This is true of many other *berachos* we recite regularly. People who have lost their appetite due to illness can appreciate the gift of being able to eat. When we recite the *berachah* for food, we should be grateful not only for having the food, but also for having a desire to eat it.

Proper concentration on the *berachos* should add simchah to our lives.

33
You Shall Be Holy

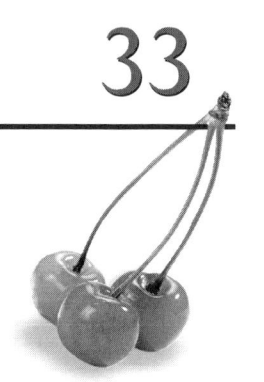

"**S**peak to the entire assembly of the Children of Israel and say to them: 'You shall be holy, for holy am I, Hashem, your G-d' " (*Leviticus* 19:2).

Just what is meant by "You shall be holy"? Rashi says that this means that one should abstain from forbidden relationships. However, inasmuch as there are specific commandments restricting these relationships, what does this commandment add?

Ramban, therefore, explains that this commandment adds a new dimension to Torah observance. We have alluded to this earlier. Holiness, Ramban says, means living a life that is thoroughly dedicated to the service of Hashem. Some people think that Torah observance is limited to the fulfillment of the positive mitzvos and avoidance of the prohibitions, but activities that are "neutral," i.e., that are neither mitzvos nor sins, are beyond the scope of Torah observance. Thus, when one partakes of a delicious meal that meets the highest standards of *kashrus,* one has certainly complied with avoidance of *tereifah* food, but one has not done a mitzvah. The fact that the food is kosher does not make its consumption a holy act.

However, if the reason a person eats is to meet the body's nutritional requirements, so that one can be in good health and thereby be able to fulfill the mitzvos, then eating the food is a necessary prerequisite for mitzvos, and it, too, becomes a mitzvah. Similarly, if one gives the body the rest that is necessary for health because one wishes to be in a condition of optimal functioning so that one can do the mitzvos properly, then rest and relaxation, too, can become mitzvos. Failure to do so diminishes the dignity of a human being, because animals, too, eat to satisfy their hunger and rest when they are weary. These activities become spiritual and uniquely human only when they are directed toward a higher goal.

The Baal Shem Tov prayed that it be revealed to him who would be his companion in *Gan Eden.* He was given the name of a person in a distant village. The Baal Shem Tov traveled to the village to meet this person, who, he felt, must be one of the hidden *tzaddikim.*

When the Baal Shem Tov met this person, he was not impressed, and after observing him for a while, he was certain that this was not a hidden *tzaddik.* The man was clearly unlearned, and there was no indication that he was particularly dedicated to performing mitzvos. The one thing the Baal Shem Tov did notice was that the man ate prodigiously, far more than normal. The Baal Shem Tov asked the man why he ate so voraciously.

The man anwered, "My father was a weak man. One time, some anti-Semitic people abducted him and ordered him to kiss a crucifix. When he refused, they beat him mercilessly, and when he could no longer withstand the beatings, he submitted.

"That will never happen to me. I eat much to make myself strong. If anyone ever dares do to me what they did to my father,

I will never submit. They will have me to contend with."

The Baal Shem Tov said that he understood why this man merited a special place in *Gan Eden*. "Why, every mouthful of food he eats is with *kiddush Hashem*, to be able to sanctify the Name of Hashem. Few people can achieve this."

While Yiddishkeit discourages asceticism, and indeed, the Talmud says that a person will be held accountable for everything he saw but did not enjoy (*Jerusalem Talmud, end of Kiddushin*), we must be careful not to slip into indulgence, and especially not to become dependent on pleasurable experiences. There is a chassidic aphorism, "What is forbidden is prohibited, and much of what is permissible is unnecessary." This can be a challenge when the kosher food industry has made so many things available. Every ethnic food and a huge variety of delicacies are available with the highest standard of kosher supervision. We must keep in mind the Ramban's interpretation of what it means to be holy.

Inasmuch as being holy is a requirement of Yiddishkeit, failure to live a holy life is a dereliction. A Jew who does not live a holy lifestyle lacks *sheleimus* (wholeness), and one cannot have simchah if one is in a state of deficiency. In contrast to those who erroneously seek happiness in pleasurable indulgences, a Jew will actually find simchah in avoiding such indulgence.

34

A Demeanor of Simchah

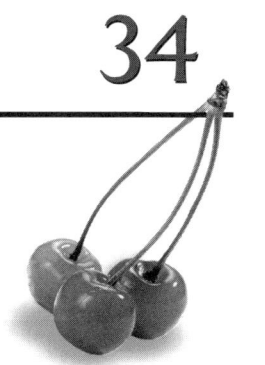

Because simchah is so central to Yiddishkeit, it is a mitzvah to cause other people to have simchah. The Talmud states that the prophet Elijah told one of the sages that two people in the market place were assured of a heavenly reward. The sage asked them what they do, and they said, "We are jesters (Rashi: We are cheerful and we cheer up others). When we see someone in the market place who is morose because he lost money, we say something to him to lift his spirits" (*Taanis* 22a). This warranted them a heavenly reward.

Earlier it was noted that Torah literature is emphatic that *atzvus* (depression) be avoided, and we pointed out that *atzvus* does not mean sadness. There are occasions when sadness is appropriate.

One of these times is when a person is aware of having sinned, which should cause him to have a *lev nishbar* (broken heart), but not *atzvus*, which is an absence of feeling. However, even when a person has a *lev nishbar*, his appearance should be cheerful. *Chovas Halevavos* says, "A pious person may have sadness (for his dereliction in *avodas Hashem*) in his heart, but his face should radiate joy."

R' Yisrael of Salant was walking to shul on Erev Yom Kippur, and met a man who did not greet him. R' Yisrael said, "It is good that you are doing *teshuvah*, but that does not warrant your showing me a gloomy disposition."

I was privileged to know the great sage of our generation, R' Shlomo Zalman Auerbach. When he died, the newspaper tried to find a photograph of him in which he was not smiling, but were unable to find one!

R' Shlomo Zalman used to say, "The problem today is that people do not share adequately in other people's simchos."

R' Shlomo Zalman never gave a newspaper interview and never allowed the press to photograph him, but was more than happy to pose for a picture with anyone who so desired. One time, when his family tried to protect him from the many callers that besieged him, he thought he saw someone standing at the door. "Please see who it is," he said to his daughter. She responded, "It's only a young boy who wants to take a picture of you." "So what is the problem?" R' Shlomo Zalman said. "Have him come in and take the picture."

Even in his illness, he did not lose his cheerful expression. "Is there anything hurting you?" his daughter asked. R' Shlomo Zalman answered jokingly, "Why do you have to know that? You're not a doctor."

One time he was walking with a friend when someone dropped a box of apples, and they scattered. R' Shlomo Zalman helped the man retrieve the apples, and the man asked, "What is your name?" "Auerbach," R' Shlomo Zalman answered. "Oh," the man said, "then you must be a relative of R' Shlomo Zalman." That's right," R' Shlomo Zalman answered. As they walked on, R' Shlomo Zalman said to his friend, "I wasn't lying. The Talmud says that a person is most closely related to himself" (*Sanhedrin* 10a).

One day he was asked to initiate the haircut of a 3-year-old child. When the father wanted to take a picture of this, R' Shlomo Zalman said, "Wait until I put on my hat and frock," and then posed for a picture with the child. A few days later the father told him that the picture had not come out. "Come back with your son," he said, "and we'll take another picture."

R' Shlomo Zalman used to say, "The Talmud quotes Shammai as saying, 'Receive every person with a cheerful face' (*Ethics of the Fathers* 1:14). R' Yishmael goes beyond that, saying, 'Receive every person with joy' (ibid. 3:16). These are halachos that we are required to observe. A gloomy expression pollutes the air. If you don't feel happy, make believe you're happy and smile."

R' Shlomo Zalman cited the Talmud, "It is greater if you cause someone to smile than if you feed him milk" (*Kesubos* 111a). "We know how great a mitzvah *tzedakah* is, yet causing another person to smile is even greater!"

R' Shlomo Zalman was very loving to children. One Shabbos night, his children brought his grandchildren for a visit. R' Shlomo Zalman gave them each some candy, and noticing the baby, he said, "Why isn't the baby smiling more?" He then played with the baby until the baby began to laugh. Only then was he satisfied.

One Shabbos, a father had arranged with the *gabbai* of the shul for his young son to chant the *haftarah,* and the child had prepared himself for this. However, one of the older worshippers insisted that he read the *haftarah,* and the disappointed child cried. Someone commented, "Where was that person's sense of propriety, to disappoint the child?" R' Shlomo Zalman remarked, "It goes even beyond a sense of propriety. An adult can forgive a slight, but a minor does not have the capacity to forgive. The man should have stepped aside in favor of the child."

If a friend of yours has a simchah — a bar mitzvah or a wedding — and you were not invited, do not feel offended. There may have been financial or space constraints that did not allow him to invite everyone. Be sure to stop off and wish him "mazal tov." It costs you nothing to add to his simchah, and it is so great a mitzvah.

35
DOING WHAT IS "FAIR AND GOOD"

Earlier it was noted that a person can fulfill the purpose for which he was created by being *yashar* (fair). Being *yashar* has halachic as well as ethical implications. Halachah requires a person who sells a property to give the right of first refusal to his neighbor. If he fails to do so and sells the property to another person, the sale can be voided (*Bava Metzia* 108a). This halachah is derived from the verse, "You shall do what is fair and good in the eyes of Hashem" (*Deuteronomy* 6:18). It is "fair and good" that the neighbor be given the opportunity to buy a property that is adjacent to his. One might argue, "Granted that perhaps it would have been a nice gesture to sell it to the neighbor if he was willing to buy it at the price it was sold to another person, but that is no reason to invalidate a legal sale." Halachah says otherwise. Failure to observe the "fair and good" provision of the Torah invalidates the sale.

In this case, the sages interpreted the verse to prescribe this halachah. However, there are many situations where *every individual* is obligated to do what is "fair and good," even if it is not stated specifically in halachah.

King Solomon says, "G-d made man just, but they (people) sought many intrigues" (*Ecclesiastes* 7:29). In a classic essay, the *mussar* authority, R' Avraham Grodzinsky, elaborates on this theme, pointing out that man was created with an innate sense of propriety and justice, and that if he fails to exercise this ability, he is derelict and culpable. Furthermore, a person cannot claim that he lacks this capacity, because inasmuch as one has the *potential*, he is derelict if he fails to develop it. R' Akiva was ignorant of Torah at the age of 40, and had he not developed himself into the great sage that he was, he would have been derelict and culpable (*Toras Avraham*).

R' Grodzinsky cites the statement that appears several times in the Talmud, "Why do we need a Scriptural source for this halachah? It is logical." In other words, a halachah that can be arrived at by sound reasoning is as binding as a Scriptural commandment (*Kesubos* 22a).

The "many intrigues" to which Solomon refers are the convoluted rationalizations whereby a person deviates from his innate sense of fairness and justice in order to satisfy his physical or ego drives. These are circuitous maneuvers, instead of the straight, simple and fair ways that are natural to a person.

In his last words, Moses says, "I have placed life and death before you, blessing and curse; and you shall choose life" (*Deuteronomy* 30:19). Who would be so foolish as to choose death and curse? The answer is that personal drives may so distort a person's judgment that one will not recognize certain behaviors as deadly and cursed. If one is able to neutralize these drives, one will, of course, choose life. Moses' warning is that we should not allow our personal drives to affect our judgment.

R' Grodzinsky's position is supported by a passage in the

Talmud. "If the Torah had not been given to us, we would have been obligated to learn respect for another's belongings by observing ants, and to learn monogamy by observing doves" (*Eruvin* 100b). Doves are monogamous, and an ant will not touch a morsel of grain that was gathered by another ant. But, without the Torah, who is to say that we would have made those observations? Perhaps we would have learned rapaciousness by observing hyenas and promiscuity by observing dogs. The answer is that even without Torah, we would have been held responsible to apply our innate sense of propriety and justice.

The Torah states that a judge who takes a bribe cannot possibly judge fairly, regardless of how much he tries. A bribe causes the judge to be "blind" to the facts of reality and to suffer a distortion of judgment (*Deuteronomy* 16:19). This applies not only to judges, but to every single individual. We constantly make judgments, and inasmuch as we are "bribed" by our personal desires, we cannot properly conduct ourselves by our own understanding of halachah. We are too vulnerable to see in halachah an approval of what we desire to do.

We are fortunate in having the Torah, which consists not only of the Scripture, but also of the Talmud and the writings of Torah scholars throughout the ages. But inasmuch as we are constantly under the influence of personal interests that constitute a "bribe," how can we possibly know that what we are doing is indeed *yashar*? R' Dessler discusses this issue in his classic essay, *Mabbat HaEmes* (Perspective of Truth, *Michtav Me'Eliyahu* vol.1 pp.52-64). He concludes that diligent study of *mussar* will enable one to avoid one's judgment being distorted.

But even with the study of *mussar*, it would be naive to assume that one can quickly achieve being *yashar*. This is a laborious task at which one must constantly work. Also, one must seek guidance from Torah scholars. Relying on one's own judgment is hazardous. "Each way of a man is right in his own eyes" (*Proverbs* 21:2), "The way of a fool is straight in his own eyes" ibid; 12:15), and "Do you see a man who is wise in his own eyes? For a fool there is more hope than for him" (ibid. 26:12). With sincere effort, and with fervent prayers to Hashem that He enlighten one to the truth, one may hope to become *yashar*.

The accounts that we have of the lives of our great Torah personalities can serve as a guide to becoming *yashar*. They were diligent not only in overcoming their personal desires, but were champions in pursuit and observance of unadulterated, uncompromising truth, always alert and sensitive to their human vulnerability of being "bribed" by personal interest.

An example of the extremes to which one must go to avoid being affected by personal interests is that of R' Moshe Zev Yaavetz, who was the rabbi and *dayan* (magistrate) of Bialystok. At that time there were two partners, Reb Zimmel Epstein and Reb Koppel Halpern, who were contractors for building the road between Moscow and Warsaw. There developed a dispute between the two, and inasmuch as they were in the vicinity of Bialystok, they decided to submit their dispute to the rabbi of Bialystok for adjudication.

When R' Moshe Zev was told that these two prominent businessmen wanted to put their case before him, he put on his *tallis*, draped it over his head, and then had the two come into his study. He addressed the men by their first names: "Zimmel and Koppel! Which of the two of you is the plaintiff?" The two were taken by surprise. No one had ever addressed them in such an unrefined way. When Reb Zimmel said that he was the plaintiff, R' Moshe said, "Zimmel, speak!" When Reb Zimmel finished, he said, "Koppel, now you speak." When Reb Koppel finished, R' Moshe Zev was silent for several minutes, then said, "According to the law of the Torah, this is my decision." After rendering his decision, he said, "Zimmel, Koppel, do you abide by my decision?" When they answered affirmatively, he lifted his *tallis*, smiled, and greeted them, "Reb Zimmel and Reb Koppel! Come with me." He then escorted them into his residence, and served them refreshments.

"You may be wondering why I behaved the way I did. The Torah says that a judge should be impartial. You are both prominent people, and I felt that if I looked at you, I might be more impressed by one of you than by the other, and that might affect my impartiality. That is why I avoided looking at you. The reason I addressed you in so crude a manner was in keeping with the Talmudic statement, 'When the litigants stand before you, think of both as being guilty' (*Ethics of the Fathers* 1:8). Now that the case has been settled, I wish to welcome you both and accord you the respect you deserve."

We may gratify a personal interest at the cost of absolute fairness, but this will frustrate our innate sense of *yashar* and prevent us from having simchah. Doing our utmost to be the *yashar* we were meant to be can lead to an enduring simchah.

36

MIDDOS

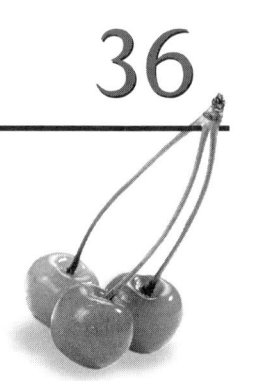

Earlier, I cited a quote from R' Chaim Vital, that *middos* (character traits) are all important and that they are, in fact, the foundation of Torah. *Nesivos Shalom* makes the following statement about *middos*:

"A person who was able to work on himself to attain the purity of *middos*, he is the truly happy person. The pure *middos* are the source of happiness in life, whereas poor *middos* impair a person's life. All the days of a person with poor *middos* are fraught with anxiety and bitterness (cf. the Talmudic statement, 'Envy, lust, and pursuit of acclaim remove a person from the world' *Ethics of the Fathers* 4:28). He is unkind to others and is constantly dissatisfied. He is intolerant of others and they do not tolerate him, so that his heart is unhappy and his life is not much of a life. On the other hand, a person who has purified his *middos* is always happy; he rejoices with others and they rejoice with him. He is the embodiment of the blessing Hashem gave to the patriarch Abraham, 'You shall *be* a blessing' (*Genesis* 12:2), his very being was a blessing, as the Midrash says, 'Whoever interacted with Abraham felt blessed' (*Bereishis Rabbah* 39). A person with pure *middos* radiates his goodness to all" (*Nesivas Shalom* vol. 1 p.76).

The principle of R' Chaim Vital can actually be found in the Talmud, which states — as noted previously — that there were several attempts to "encapsulate" the Torah. The first attempt, the Talmud says, was by King David, who condensed the Torah into eleven principles. "O G-d, who shall dwell in Your tent, who shall rest on Your holy mountain? One who walks in perfect innocence, and does what is right, and speaks truth from his heart; who has no slander on his tongue, who has done his fellow no evil, nor cast disgrace upon his close one; in whose eyes a contemptible person is repulsive, but who honors those who fear Hashem; who can swear to his own detriment without retracting; who lends not his money on interest; nor takes a bribe against the innocent" (*Psalms* 15:1-5). The prophet Isaiah summarized Torah in six principles. "One who walks righteously, speaks justly, rejects unfair profit, refuses to hear (accept) innocent bloodshed, diverts his eyes from improper gazing" (3:15). The prophet Micah reduced Torah to three concepts. "What is it that G-d asks of you? To do justice, love lovingkindness, and walk humbly with G-d" (6:8). The prophet Habbakuk summarized Torah in a single statement. "The righteous shall live by faith" (2:4; *Makkos* 33b).

When the proselyte asked Hillel to teach him the entire Torah while he was standing on one foot, Hillel said, "Do not do to another person anything that you would not want done to you.. That is the essence of Torah. The rest is commentary, which you must learn" (*Shabbos* 31b). Rabbi Akiva echoed Hillel's opinion when he said, "The all-encompassing principle of Torah is, 'Love your fellow as yourself' " (*Jerusalem Talmud,Nedarim* 9:4). Ben Zoma said that the all-encompassing principle of Torah is contained in the verse, "This is the book of the history of man, on the day G-d created earth and heaven" (*Genesis* 5:1). Bar Kapara said that the verse, "Know Him in all your ways" (*Proverbs* 3:6), is "a small portion upon which the entire Torah is based" (*Berachos* 36a)

These varying opinions really do not differ in substance, and are merely different ways in which these authorities express the same concept on the essence of Torah.

The Torah states that man was created in "the likeness of G-d" (*Bereishis* 5:1). Inasmuch as G-d has no image, we must understand this "likeness" to mean that one should have the Divine attributes. "Just as G-d is merciful, so must man be merciful" (*Shabbos* 133b). Here, too, we see that the ultimate perfection of man is to have proper *middos*.

It is the *yetzer hara* that seeks to corrupt man and divert him from proper *middos*. The Talmud quotes G-d as saying, "I did indeed create the *yetzer hara*, but I created Torah as its antidote" (*Kiddushin* 30b). Precisely because *middos* are the foundation of Torah, the *yetzer hara* directs its attack on *middos* more than on any other facet of Yiddishkeit. Because bad *middos* tend to become engrained in a person's character, it requires great effort to extirpate them.

Although the proper *middos* are described in many of the Torah writings, beginning with the Talmudic volume, *Ethics of the Fathers*, to the contemporary *mussar* authorities, our understanding of them is inadequate unless we can see how our great Torah personalities lived and how they implemented the *middos*. Otherwise, the effect of these writings is similar to lecturing to children. Indeed, knowledge of how our *tzaddikim* lived their lives may surpass in effectiveness the academic knowledge of Torah. The Midrash states that "the conversation of the servants of the patriarchs is superior to the Torah knowledge of their descendants" (*Bereishis Rabbah* 60:8). This is because the description of how the patriarchs acted is the most effective way of our understanding the behavior that the Torah requires of us.

The Talmudic volume, *Ethics of the Fathers*, begins with the receiving of the Torah by Moses, and continues with its transmission to Joshua and then to an uninterrupted chain of Talmudic sages. Following closure of the Talmud, the transmission of Torah ethics has continued via the Torah personalities who, in their lives, incorporated *middos* whose origin was ultimately in the Divine ethical teachings given to Moses. Incorporating Torah ethics in behavior is as essential to Yiddishkeit as observance of the ritual mitzvos.

We are fortunate in having accounts of the *middos* of the *tzaddikim* of yore, as well as eyewitness accounts of the *middos* of *tzaddikim* close to our own time. They embodied the teachings of Sinai, and it is from their lives that we can learn what constitutes a "kingdom of priests and a holy nation." We will draw upon the great works of *mussar* and *chassidus* as well as on the biographies of our *tzaddikim* to enable us to understand what is authentic Yiddishkeit, as Solomon said, "*deracheha darchei noam, v'chal nesivoseha shalom,* the ways of Torah are pleasant, and all its paths are peaceful" (*Proverbs* 3:17).

Although there may be several approaches to the philosophy of *middos*, they ultimately merge into a common path and goal. For example, we have cited the Talmud, that a person should emulate the Divine *middos*, "As He is compassionate, so should you be compassionate. As He is merciful, so should you be merciful" (*Shabbos* 133b). The Torah tells us that we are to "cleave unto Hashem," and this is accomplished by emulating the Divine *middos*. *Tanya* cites the *Zohar* (*Acharei* 73) that "the Torah, Hashem, and Israel are a single unit," and the Talmud quotes Hashem as saying that He incorporated Himself in the Torah (*Shabbos* 105a). Therefore, *Tanya* says that when one embraces Torah *middos*, one is embracing and uniting with Hashem.

The gravity of improper *middos* can be seen from the following anecdote. When R' Yisrael of Salant was in Vilna, an incident occurred that shocked him. A shoemaker, who was one of the lesser luminaries in the community, inherited wealth from a relative, and when he married off his daughter, he did so in grandiose style. One person, who was irritated by this "upstart" who was flaunting his wealth, approached him as the wedding party was marching down the street, handed him a pair of shoes and said,

"Can you repair these by tomorrow?" R' Yisrael said that at that point, all the great rabbis who had served in Vilna in the past were called out of *Gan Eden* to appear before the Heavenly Tribunal, which held them accountable for this terrible humiliation. As rabbis of Vilna, they should have instilled better *middos* in their constituents, which in turn should have prevented this humiliating act.

Particular caution to avoid offending someone must be taken at home, between husband and wife, where the familiarity in the relationship may cause one to lower one's guard. The Talmud says that a husband should take great care not to cause his wife anguish, because women are more emotionally sensitive and are easily moved to tears, and a husband will be held accountable for aggrieving her (*Bava Metzia* 59a). R' Chaim Vital says that if a person relates disrespectfully to his wife, all his merits may be discounted.

The following anecdote indicates the importance our Torah personalities accorded to being sensitive to other people's feelings, and going to extremes to avoid even remotely offending someone.

R' Moshe Kliers, rabbi of Tiberias, was friendly with the rabbi of the Sephardic community. People told him that the *eruv* (symbolic fence that permits carrying objects in the street on Shabbos) that the Sephardic rabbi had devised was problematic. R' Moshe ruled that the *eruv* was kosher.

On Sunday, R' Moshe visited the Sephardic rabbi and said, "I have a problem understanding a difficult portion of the Talmud. Perhaps you can help me." The Sephardic rabbi said, "Surely you jest. You do not expect me to explain Talmud to you."

"I may have some kind of mental block," R' Moshe said. "If you will learn this portion with me, I may understand it better."

R' Moshe then showed the rabbi the Talmudic passage in the Talmud that related to the laws of *eruv*. The rabbi exclaimed, "Oh! I erred in the construction of the *eruv*." R' Moshe smiled. "That is why I came. I wanted you to correct your judgment."

"How did you rule about the *eruv* on this Shabbos?" the rabbi asked.

"I ruled that it was kosher," R' Moshe said.

"But why?" the rabbi asked. "You knew that it was problematic."

R' Moshe said, "Yes, but at the very worst, an improper *eruv* can result in violating a rabbinic ordinance. Had I ruled that *eruv* you designed was not valid, that would have been an insult to you and to your position as a Torah authority, and that would have been a violation of a much more serious, Scriptural prohibition."

Another example. When the son of R' Eliezer Yehudah Finkel, Rosh Yeshivah of Mir, was having a *bris* for his child, they gave the honor of *sandek* to his uncle, R' Avraham Shmuel Finkel, son of the Elder of Slabodka. The honor of being *sandek* is generally given to the most spiritual person present, and R' Avraham Shmuel was certainly the appropriate choice for *sandek*.

The honor of being *kvatter* (bringing in the infant) was given to a distant relative from Germany who was visiting. When they announced this guest's name as *kvatter*, they were astonished to see him stride to the seat designated for the *sandek* and take his place there. The reason for this was that in Germany, the term *kvatter* is actually used for whom we call the *sandek*, and this guest assumed that he had been designated as the *sandek*. Understandably, he was not in the league of R' Avraham Shmuel, and the logical thing would have been to explain the misunderstanding to him.

R' Avraham Shmuel understood what had happened, and did not permit anyone to say a word. He stood by quietly, as the baby was placed on the guest's lap, and the latter served as *sandek*. To have explained the misunderstanding would have meant that the guest would have had to vacate the *sandek* chair, and that would have been embarrassing to him. Avoiding humiliation was far more important than having the most spiritual person as *sandek*.

In Chapter 6 of *Ethics of the Fathers*, the Talmud lists no less than 48 *middos* traits that are essential for the acquisition of Torah. It follows that anyone bereft of these traits can hardly be considered a true Torah scholar, and that a person who possesses these traits is not only a Torah scholar but also a highly refined, spiritual person.

Some character traits, such as "Do not have hatred for your fellow in your heart," or "Love your fellow as yourself," deal with emotions. One might ask: Can emotions be legislated? It is one thing to be told to abstain from eating *tereifah* or working on Shabbos. These are *actions* that a person can control. But to love or not to hate — are these within voluntary control so that one can be ordered to observe them?

The answer is that a person *can* indeed exert control over feelings. *Tanya* says that it is inborn within a human being that the intellect can be master over the affects. It may take more effort than one is willing to exert, but a person does have control over his feelings.

You may say, "True, but that is something that only great *tzaddikim* can achieve. I am not capable of controlling how I should feel."

There is a method that is practical for everyone. If you dislike someone, *do something nice for him*. In a classic essay, Rav Dessler says that the commonly held idea that we give to those whom we love is erroneous. Just the opposite is true. *You love those to whom you give.* When you do favors for someone, you get to like him (*Michtav Me'Eliyahu* vol.1, pp. 35-36).

This principle is stated by Ramchal in *Mesilas Yesharim* (Path of the Just). "*External behavior determines internal feelings*" (Chapter 7). This is the dynamics of Rav Dessler's principle. Behave *as though* you like the person, and you will get to like him.

"But how can I act lovingly toward a person whom I hate?" Very simple. Just do it. It may not be easy, and you may not *want* to do it, but you *can* do it. A person may not want to abstain from food on Yom Kippur, but we do so because we are commanded to. Similarly, you may not want to do a kindness to someone you dislike, but you should do it because the Torah demands it of you.

There is yet another approach to take charge of one's feelings. Ramban begins the letter to his son by instructing him to avoid rage. (As we shall subsequently see, "rage" is not the same as "anger.") Ramban then goes on to say that refraining from rage will bring a person to *humility*, which is the finest of all *middos*.

The obvious question is: If humility is the finest of all *middos*, why did Ramban not begin his letter with humility? Why did he begin by discouraging rage, which will then lead to humility? The answer is that humility is a *feeling*, and it is indeed difficult to initiate a feeling. Ramban, therefore, begins with an *action*, which is more readily subject to control. It may indeed be difficult to restrain oneself from rage when provoked, but it is nevertheless within one's means to suppress an action.

There are traits which, like light and darkness, are mutually exclusive. A person may notice that a living-room chair is shabby, and replace it with a new one. But now the sofa, in contrast to the new chair, is very unattractive. One, therefore, buys a new sofa. However, the old carpet clashes with the chair and sofa. The carpet is replaced, and then the pictures, drapes, and lamps are brought into harmony. The entire room underwent a total overhaul that may never have been intended, but resulted from bringing in one new chair.

If a person refrains from responding angrily when provoked, that refines one's character. Indeed, the Talmud gives this person the highest praise, as one who is beloved by Hashem (*Pesachim* 113b). Other negative traits now become incompatible with this refined character, and as with the room that ultimately undergoes a complete change, a total overhaul of character may result from changing just one trait.

Of course, it is possible that Ramban began with restraining one's expression of anger rather than with humility, because the former is a greater challenge. The Torah says of Moses that he was the "most humble person on the face of the earth" (*Numbers* 12:3), yet, the Talmud points out that Moses erred as a result of becoming enraged (*Vayikra Rabbah* 13:1). Even the most spiritual person is vulnerable to losing control of his anger.

Elsewhere (*Lights Along the Way* p.68) I have pointed out that there may be some confusion about anger because the same Hebrew word, *kaas,* is used for three distinctive phases of anger.

(1) *Kaas* is the *feeling* of anger when one is provoked or offended. This feeling is innate and is difficult to extirpate, as indicated by the fact that the Chafetz Chaim prayed fervently for Hashem to rid him of the feeling of anger. The Chafetz Chaim's *middos* were exemplary. No one ever saw him express anger, because that was something he could control. Not to *feel* anger when provoked is beyond one's control, and one must pray to Hashem to be free from it.

(2) *Kaas* is the *reaction* when one feels anger, and this is well within one's control. It is the loss of control that the Talmud condemns, so far as to equate rage with idolatry. Of rage the Talmud says that it deprives a prophet of his prophetic powers and a wise person of his wisdom (*Pesahim 66b*).

R' Chaim Vital said, "My teacher (the Ari *z"l*) was more demanding about rage than all other sins, even if one is angry for the sake of a mitzvah.He would say that all other sins affect only a part of the *neshamah*, whereas rage affects the entire *neshamah* and renders it *tereifah*" (*Shaar Ruach HaKodesh*).

During a cholera epidemic, R' Yisrael of Salant told his students that on Shabbos they should do whatever is necessary for the sick person, because the restrictions of Shabbos are suspended in a case of *pikuach nefesh* (danger to life). One person remarked to R' Yisrael that he felt the students were taking too many liberties with this suspension of restrictions. R' Yisrael shouted at him, "You are going to teach me the halachos of Shabbos? I am responsible for these people's lives!" R' Yisrael later explained that he had to react forcefully because this was said in the presence of some students, who might have hesitated in attending to the sick on Shabbos. Nevertheless, for the rest of his life R' Yisrael was bothered that he had acted in rage, albeit justified.

"A person who restrains his anger will never regret it" (*Sefer HaYashar of Rabbeinu Tam, Shaar* 6). How true. One need only think of the incidents where one lost one's temper. Almost without exception, one later thinks, *I wish I had not said that.* Controlling one's rage is conducive to simchah, because one does not have severe recriminations.

(3) *Kaas* is harboring resentments or holding a grudge. Although one may not have control over feeling angry at the moment of provocation, he can divest himself of the anger. Retaining anger is a violation of "You shall not hate your brother in your heart" (*Leviticus* 19:17), and it is of this phase of *kaas* that Solomon says, "Anger lingers in the bosom of fools" (*Ecclesiastes* 7:9). To allow anger to linger is indeed foolish.

The folly of harboring resentments is easily understood. The Torah explicitly forbids not only taking revenge and refusing to do someone a favor that one would normally have done, but also doing the favor and saying, "I'm doing this for you even though you don't deserve it because you did not help me when I needed it" (*Leviticus* 19:18). Inasmuch as one is forbidden to act out one's resentment in any way, of what purpose can it be to harbor it? It is not only a totally useless feeling, but also one that is self-destructive. The person you resent couldn't care less how you feel about him. He does not suffer from insomnia or indigestion. *You* are the one who is suffering from the resentment. Is it not foolish for you to suffer because the other person behaved badly?

"Those who are insulted and do not return an insult, who hear themselves being humiliated and do not respond, of them it is said, 'Those who love Hashem are like the sun at its mightiest' " (*Shabbos* 88b). Joseph's brothers committed a heinous act, selling him into slavery, yet he completely forgave them, and tried to alleviate their guilt by saying, " Now, do not be distressed nor reproach yourself for having sold me here, for it was to be a provider that Hashem sent me ahead of you. It was not you who sent me here, but Hashem" (*Genesis* 44:5-8). "He comforted them and spoke to their heart."

"Listen, O Shepherd of Israel, You who leads Joseph like a flock" (*Psalms* 80:2). Why do we invoke the merit of Joseph? Because we pray to Hashem that just as Joseph behaved with kindness toward his brothers who had dealt so cruelly with him, so Hashem should overlook our misdeeds and treat us with kindness

(*Yalkut*). "One who overlooks a personal affront is forgiven all his sins" (*Rosh Hashanah* 17a). "This trait can add years to a person's life, even if it had been decreed that he die" (*Shemiras Halashon, Shaar* 2:8). How right Solomon was, that resentments are the greatest folly! By divesting oneself of resentments one can merit forgiveness of one's sins and gain long life. This is reason for simchah.

Envy is another trait that is both useless and self-destructive. Here, too, one may ask: How can I be ordered not to be envious? If another person can afford comforts and luxuries that I cannot afford, can I help being envious of him?

There are several answers to this. An anecdotal answer is provided by R' Yitzchok Silberstein in *Aleinu L'Shabeiach*. A man complained that he cannot overcome his envy of a neighbor who always buys the latest model car, whereas his car spends more time in the repair shop than on the road. R' Silberstein said, "Unless I am mistaken, your neighbor suffers from stomach ulcers, doesn't he? If you want what he has, you must accept *everything* he has. It comes in a package." R' Silberstein continued, "Perhaps we may read that into the words of the Torah. 'Do not covet your fellow's wife, manservant, nor *all* that he has' (*Exodus* 20:14). If you want the good he has, you must accept the bad that he has as well."

Ibn Ezra gives this explanation. A person would never covet something that is absolutely beyond his reality of getting. Thus, a peasant would never think of marrying a princess. (Or, another example: the greediest person in the world would not think of obtaining the gold and jewels on a star millions of light-years distant.) If someone is truly committed to the other commandments, so that stealing, killing, or committing adultery is an absolute impossibility for him, he would never covet anything his neighbor possesses. In other words, "You shall not covet" is not really a commandment. Rather, it is a statement of fact. If one is totally committed to the observance of the other commandments, the natural consequence will be that one will not covet.

As with harboring resentments, envy is self-destructive. An envious person cannot be happy because he is chronically dissatisfied with whatever he has. An envious person cannot enjoy life.

This can have deleterious physical as well as psychological effects. Solomon stated this well, "Envy is the rot of the bones" (*Proverbs* 14:30).

There is a prayer at the close of the *Amidah,* that "we should not envy others, nor should others envy us." Why should we pray for others not to be envious of us? This is to remind us that we should not flaunt what we have, which may cause distress to others.

R' Avigdor Miller said that the reason an *ayin hara* (evil eye) may have a deleterious effect is because by displaying one's good fortune, one may cause those who have less to feel bad, and it is a sin to cause another person pain of any kind.

Inasmuch as envy is both useless and destructive, why did Hashem instill this trait in people? It is because it has a positive use if one envies people who are more learned and more spiritual. "Envy of scholars increases wisdom" (*Bava Basra* 21a). Like so many other things in the world that can have both positive and negative applications, there is a place for constructive envy.

If one were asked, What is the greatest danger to one's spiritual well-being? One might answer, "living in a corrupt environment," or "associating with evil people." These are no doubt very harmful. However, Ramchal says of *indolence* that "there is nothing as dangerous as the danger of indolence" (*Mesilas Yesharim* 7). It is known that the Vilna Gaon said of *Mesilas Yesharim* that "in the first nine chapters there is not a single superfluous letter." That means that Ramchal's statement, "there is nothing as dangerous as the danger of indolence," must be taken literally, and not just as a dramatic expression.

The Midrash says that on every blade of grass there is an angel that commands "Grow!" (*Bereishis Rabbah* 10:7). Why must a blade of grass be ordered to grow? It has air, water, and all the necessary nutrients. It is just natural that it should grow, isn't it? The Midrash is telling us that *inertia* is the natural state of all matter, and that without being commanded to grow, the grass seed would do nothing.

Ramchal states that inasmuch as man was formed out of earth, his natural state is indolence. Any action whatsoever requires a motivation strong enough to thwart one's very nature. Any motion, any act, must of necessity overcome the resistance of inertia.

Because motivation is necessary to overcome the natural state of "doing nothing," the human organism ingeniously seeks to avoid the discomfort of overpowering the natural state by neutralizing the motivation. It does so by garnering a variety of rationalizations to justify doing nothing. Nowhere is this described more accurately than in *Proverbs* (22:13, 26:13-16). "The lazy man says, 'There is a lion outside. I shall be murdered in the streets.' The lazy man says, "There is a jackal on the path, a lion in the streets. The door is already turning on its hinges, and the sluggard is still on his bed. *The lazy man is wiser in his own eyes than seven sensible counselors."* This last sentence is an important psychological fact. The lazy person is absolutely convinced that his reasoning is correct, and even seven wise counselors cannot budge him from his opinion.

The danger in indolence is further stated by Solomon. "I passed by a field of a lazy man, and by the vineyard of a man devoid of understanding, and I saw everything come up in thistles; the surface was covered with thorns, and the stone wall was torn down. This I saw and set my heart to it, I saw it and learned the lesson. *Yet a little sleep, a little slumber, a little folding of the hands to rest, and your poverty will stalk you; your want will come as an armed man"* (*Proverbs* 24:30-34).

Another very important principle is contained in the last verse. One does not see the danger of just "a little sleep, a little slumber, a little folding of the hands to rest," and is not aware that the consequences will be the utter ruination of his field, vineyard, or whatever else is contingent on his actions. It is so *easy* to procrastinate. A person can easily convince himself that there is ample time to take care of matters later, and that he may have just a few more minutes of rest. It is because of this self-deception that Ramchal says, "there is nothing as dangerous as the danger of indolence." A person who commits a sin generally does not deceive himself the way one does when procrastinating. Indolence should be thought of as a passive sin, but a sin nevertheless.

Among the positive *middos* is *empathy*. The ethicist, R' Yeruchem Levovitz, says that not only is empathy a mitzvah, it is the basis for all the mitzvos between man and fellow man, and probably also between man and G-d. The source for this mitzvah is the verse in the Torah that Moses went out among his brethren and "he saw in their burdens" (*Exodus* 2:11), upon which the Midrash comments that Moses wept with them, and *put his shoulder under the burden to carry it with them,* saying, "I wish I would die instead of you" (*Shemos Rabbah* 1:25). R' Yeruchem said that neither crying for them nor saying, "I wish I would die instead of you," constitutes true empathy. It was only when Moses put his shoulder under the burden and felt what the Israelites were feeling that he empathized with them (*Daas Chochmah U'Mussar,* vol. 4 p. 29:32).

Empathizing with another person's distress is painful, and our natural instinct is to avoid pain. One must, therefore, make a concerted effort to overcome this resistance and feel the other person's suffering. Relieving another's suffering is a kind of simchah to that person as well as to oneself.

A chassid once came to his Rebbe, complaining of his bitter poverty, and pleading with the Rebbe to give him a *berachah* for prosperity. The Rebbe said, "I will give you a *berachah,* provided that you follow my instructions to the letter." The chassid agreed he would do so.

The Rebbe gave the chassid some money and said, "You must do exactly as I say. With this money you are to buy the finest delicacies, take them home, and eat them in the presence of your wife and children. Under no circumstances may you give them even the tiniest morsel of your food. After you do this, come back to me."

The chassid followed instructions, and his hungry children sat around the table, their mouths watering, looking longingly at the food their father was eating which he would not share with them. Each bite of food he took was torture. How could he eat when his children were starving? It would have been easier for him to swallow rocks rather than roast meat.

When he returned, the Rebbe said, "You could not partake of

the food when your children were starving. How will you be able to enjoy wealth when you know that there are poor people who lack the basics of life? But you asked for wealth, and wealth you shall have."

The chassid returned home and had phenomenal success. Whatever he bought, the price skyrocketed and he sold it at a huge profit. In time he became wealthy. He built a *hachnassas orchim* (hospitality house) for the homeless, and a huge soup kitchen. He often slept in the *hachnassas orchim* and shared the meals in the soup kitchen. He had learned to empathize.

R' Yeruchem points out that fulfillment of the many mitzvos that govern interpersonal relationships is impossible without empathy. With empathy, one can be courteous, considerate, patient, honest, respectful, and self-sacrificing. The mitzvah of empathy is unparalleled in refining a person's character.

As was noted, the common effort to achieve happiness via gratification of one's desires is nothing but self-deception. Whereas deceiving someone else is ethically wrong, deceiving oneself is simply foolish. Success at self-deception is the greatest failure.

One of the self-deceptive traits is procrastination. *Mesilas Yesharim* states that procrastination is "the greatest of all dangers." If a person decides that he will not do something, at least he knows where he stands. If he denies that he will not do it, but says, "I will do it later," he is deceiving no one but himself. That is why procrastination is one of the worst *middos*. It is obvious that postponing something that one should be doing is going to interfere with the achievement necessary for simchah.

It should be obvious that improving one's *middos* is a sure way of attaining simchah, not only the simchah of spiritual growth, but also the simchah of happiness.

37

DOES MOURNING NEGATE SIMCHAH?

We hope and pray to be spared from loss of loved ones, but the reality is that one will invariably experience the death of a loved one. At one *shivah* call, a visitor said to the mourner, "May you never know of any mourning again." The mourner responded, "Why are you cursing me? My father is alive, and it would be a terrible tragedy if I died during his lifetime. The natural order of things is for children to survive their parents, and all children will have to mourn a parent. To wish someone otherwise is hardly a blessing."

As was noted, one of the interpretations of simchah is *lev shalem*, to accept adversity with trust in the wisdom of Hashem. Inasmuch as mourning is unavoidable, it is important that we understand how the halachos of mourning are helpful so that mourning does not negate simchah.

Although mourning is necessary, it must be confined so that it does not interfere with ongoing life. The death of a loved one is certainly painful, but one must seek closure.

We live in a culture that tends to deny death, as is evident from the exorbitant prices people pay for a coffin — quilted at that — as though the person who had passed away could be physically made more comfortable. Euphemisms are frequently used to avoid the term "dead." A cemetery may be the most beautiful area in the community. (A visitor to Japan asked a mourner who placed a bowl of rice on the grave, "Just when do you think your relative is going to eat that?" The man responded, "When your relatives smell the flowers you put on their graves.") One of the cruelest examples of denial of death occurs in some hospitals, where a terminally ill patient is isolated to avoid anyone being present at the time of death.

The problem with this is that we must live in a real world, and the refusal to accept reality may cause serious psychological problems. Well-intending relatives may procure tranquilizers for a grieving spouse, purportedly to mitigate his/her grief. This may result in unresolved grief, which can cause serious emotional consequences that may be difficult to treat. Not infrequently, they may seek to tranquilize the mourner because of their own discomfort in seeing him/her cry and grieve.

The laws of mourning are too extensive to enumerate here, but their general effect is to enable the person to accept death as a reality, to bring closure to a cherished relationship, so that surviviors can then be able to go on with life. During the *shivah,* the mourners may not distract themselves by working. They are visited by friends, many of whom knew the person who died, and they may share memories with the mourners. The mourning period of 30 days is less intense, as are the 12 months following the death of a parent.

The mourner's prayer, *Kaddish,* is singular in that it makes no reference to death. Rather, the emphasis is on bringing greater glory to the Name of Hashem. The way to honor a dead relative is to live one's life properly.

Solomon says, "It is better to go to the house of mourning than to the house of feasting, for that is the end of all man, and the living should take it to heart" (*Ecclesiastes* 7:2). It has been wisely said that some people live as though they will never die, and die as though they had never lived. We are successful in putting thoughts of death out of our minds, sometimes living at a frenetic pace and behaving as though we would live forever. Awareness of one's mortality may make one reflect on what one should accomplish in a lifetime. "The living should take it to heart."

The occurrence of a death may at least, momentarily shake a person loose from denial, and cause one to think about the meaning of life. Furthermore, when one sees how a departed person is remembered, one might think, *How do I wish to be remembered?* Before doing a particular act, one might think, *Would I wish to be remembered as having done this?*

One mourner, who read the translation of *Kaddish,* said, "It made me understand that every person has a mission in life to bring honor and glory to G-d. But no one is perfect. By saying *Kaddish,* I commit myself to try to carry out the mission that my father did not have the opportunity to complete."

The death of a loved one is understandably an impediment to happiness, but need not be an impediment to simchah and eventual restoration of happiness.

Epilogue

Travelers in the desert, when their throats are parched for water, may see a mirage, an oasis where they will be able to get lifesaving water. When they arrive at the "oasis," they are bitterly disappointed to discover that it was nothing but a hallucination. Their intense desire for water, coupled with some climatic conditions of the desert, result in a hallucination.

Much the same can be said of the universal quest for happiness. The intense desire, coupled with some circumstances or events in the outside world, give rise to a hallucinated happiness. Unfortunately, when one arrives at the hallucinated happiness, one is either totally disappointed to discover that there is nothing there, and if one should experience a brief moment of pleasure, it soon dissipates and one then awaits another hallucination, always thinking that this one is real.

It has been said that "insanity consists of doing the same thing and expecting different results." People who cannot control their weight may repeatedly try "miracle diets," guaranteed to reduce weight rapidly. Logical thinking would tell them that with 10 or more "miracle diets" appearing every month year in and year out, none of these could be sustained over a longer period of time. Nevertheless, they try again, because hope springs eternal in the human breast. "None of the 20 others I tried worked, but this one will be different."

Logical thinking would tell people that inasmuch as all the searches for happiness that they pursued in the past were disappointing, they ought to change course. But no, like the dieter, they deceive themselves to believe that gratification of their next desire will make them happy. The Midrash says that no person ever leaves this world with even half of his desires gratified (*Koheles Rabbah* 1:34). This pursuit is futile.

Although simchah can mean happiness, we have seen that it can have several other meanings. Indeed, the "happiness" aspect of simchah is contingent on the fulfillment of all the other meanings. Furthermore, in contrast to a mirage where the hallucination is the goal, in simchah it is the *process* rather than any goal that constitutes simchah. Hence, simchah is not always euphoric, and its attainment may demand much effort.

It stands to reason that an unfulfilled person cannot be truly happy. We have noted that whereas one comes into the world with only animalistic desires, one achieves an identity as a human being only by subjugating these desires and striving for spiritual perfection. As R' Elimelech of Lizhensk says, "A person was created to transform himself." Pursuit of physical desires frustrates the very purpose of one's being, and that defeats the attainment of simchah.

King Solomon says, "Hashem made man *yashar* (straight, simple), but man sought many calculations" (*Ecclesiastes* 7:29). The *yashar* person is the one who seeks to participate in his own creation, as was explained regarding "Let us make man." The calculations that divert a person from being *yashar* are the self-centered behaviors that characterize subhuman creatures.

This is why King David says, "*Le'yishrei lev simchah*" (Psalms 97:11). Those who are truly *yashar* in heart are the ones who attain simchah.

Ironically, many people who think they are pursuing happiness are actually fleeing from it.

Simchah is attainable, but we must know what simchah is and where to look for it. Hopefully this book has provided the tools that will make this search productive and fruitful.